CW00607305

WHOSE SIDE ARE THEY ON?

How Big-Brother
Government is ruining Britain

Alan Pearce

www.alanpearce.com

GIBSON SQUARE

For Tom & Barry

Also by Alan Pearce:

www.alanpearce.com
It's Health and Safety Gone Mad
Whose Side Are They On

This title first published in 2009 by

Gibson Square, London

UK Tel: +44 (0)20 7096 1100
Fax: +44 (0)20 7993 2214

US Tel: +1 646 216 9813
Fax: +1 646 216 9488

Eire Tel: +353 (0)1 657 1057

rights@gibsonsquare.com
www.gibsonsquare.com

ISBN 9 7 8 1 9 0 6 1 4 2 5 0 6

Printed by Clays, Bungay.

PREFACE

THE DEATH OF COMMON SENSE

What on earth have we been thinking? We claim to live in a democracy and yet we let the government walk all over us. We swallow ministerial statements on terrorism, bankers and knife crime as if they were gospel and we allow ourselves to be filmed and followed wherever we go.

Today, the State has carte blanche to read our emails and track us online. They can tap our telephones, enter our homes, bug our offices and sift through our bins.

Tough anti-terror laws ensure 'bin criminals' and school catchment cheats are punished while on-the-spot fines keep us all in line. These days we need police approval to protest and will shortly need permission to leave the country.

Our biometric data – said to protect us from terrorists and organised crime – is openly shared with sinister bio-tech industries. And, while billions are wasted on government databases, they can't keep the most basic information secure.

Our children are demonised and isolated from society. We moan that they 'hang about' our streets and then make it next to impossible for adults to supervise their hobbies and sports activities. After more than a decade of New Labour, more teenagers are leaving school without even the most basic qualifications.

We treat our returning soldiers worse than the Victorians to the point where they must rely on charity for their welfare rather than receive sufficient help from a grateful State. Our Iraq and Afghan veterans now form the largest single group by profession in our over-crowded jails.

And yet we tolerate politicians on the take and don't bat an eyelid when they champion ID cards and then draw additional pay from companies bidding for the contract. Hello David Blunkett.

Knee-jerk politicians have doomed our traditional way of life, rights and freedoms. We have joined the ranks of the repressive regimes with our control orders, house arrest, detention without trial, and secret evidence and secret trials. What were once seen as intolerable affronts to human dignity are now regarded as necessary tools in the fight for freedom in 21st-century Britain.

It may all be for our own good or it might just be the end of British democracy and the death of common sense.

If the government are not on our side, we really should ask Whose side are they on?

Alan Pearce
www.alanpearce.com

'The government that governs best,
governs least'

Thomas Paine

'If you have 10,000 regulations,
you destroy all respect for the law'

Winston Churchill

1

EASY TARGETS

'Tough on crime, tough on the causes of crime' – Tony Blair.

GARETH CORKHILL is the kind of criminal that the government has squarely in its sights. He was easy to arrest and easy to prosecute. His conviction acted as a deterrent to others contemplating similar crimes. He made national headlines soon after officers in body armour apprehended him at his home. Gareth Corkhill had left the lid of his wheelie bin open four inches.

He now has a criminal record which bars him from ever visiting countries such as the United States and Canada. He must disclose his shady past every time he applies for a new job and if he wants credit or seeks a mortgage. His fingerprints and DNA will be kept on file long after his death. He was also obliged to contribute financially to a fund for victims of violence.

Gareth Corkhill, a bus driver and father of four from Whitehaven in Cumbria, is one of 20,000 homeowners fined for 'bin crimes' in a 12 month period. And in the government's fight against crime his is a success story.

Bin criminals now pay higher fines – up to £30 more – than those of shoplifters and offensive drunks.

Local government spokesman for the Conservatives, Eric Pickles, says New Labour has created an army of municipal bin bullies who target law-abiding families with massive fines while professional criminals get the kid gloves.

'It's clear Whitehall bureaucrats are instructing town halls to

target householders with fines for minor breaches,' he says. 'Yet
with the slow death of weekly collections and shrinking bins, it is
increasingly hard for families to dispose of their rubbish
responsibly. It is fundamentally unfair that householders are now
getting hammered with larger fines than shoplifters.'

Fear of recycling

MAGISTRATES fined Swansea journalist Michael Reeves £200
after finding him guilty of putting an item of junk mail in a
recycling sack for bottles and cans – breaking council rules.

The court was told the letter, which was addressed to him,
'contaminated' the other items put out for recycling. After the
hearing Mr Reeves said he had since stopped recycling and feared
his case would discourage others.

Mr Reeves was earlier served with a warning notice when he
put his bins out a day early because he was going on holiday. Then
two months later a green recycling bag was found outside his
ground floor flat containing paper and bottles and cans.

Swansea Council enforcement officer Martin Lemon said:
'The fly-tipping team have responsibility for collecting waste that
has been incorrectly disposed of. The teams are trained to search
through any offending waste that they have found to look for
evidence of its origins.'

The sports writer with the city's *Evening Post* newspaper denied
putting the letter in the bag. The court heard there were no eye
witnesses or camera footage of him doing so. His solicitor Nicola
Smith said there was 'an array' of possibilities of how it came to
be in the sack.

But magistrates found him guilty and fined him £100 and
ordered him to pay £100 costs.

'I don't believe they proved beyond reasonable doubt that I
put the paper in the bag – I did not,' said Mr Reeves. 'I have not
recycled since I received the summons. People are not going to
recycle if they end up in court and it costs them £200.'

If at first you don't succeed

WHEN Exeter Council failed in its bid to prosecute Donna Challice for putting food and cigarette ends in her green bin they just changed the rules.

Now anyone in the borough putting inappropriate waste into a green bin will be sent a £70 fixed-penalty notice to compensate the council for cleaning it. Those who refuse to pay will be taken to court and prosecuted for non-payment. Other councils are expected to follow suit.

The 32-year-old mother-of-three was earlier found not guilty after the court ruled the council had been unable to prove she put the waste into the bin herself.

Mike Trim, the council's cleansing services head, said the prosecution failed because the court required evidence from eye witnesses or CCTV.

'Now if we find a contaminated bin under the terms of Section 46 of the Environmental Protection Act we serve a notice on every adult person in the household concerned,' he explained.

The move came just weeks after it was revealed that house-holders face on-the-spot fines of up to £110 for overfilling their bins under a government instruction to local authorities.

Fined for putting rubbish in bin

BOSTON Council fined a pensioner £75 for putting rubbish in a litter bin on a lamp post. John Richards, 84, was traced from his address on an envelope in the plastic bag with the household scraps.

He said he did not want to wait for the council's fortnightly collection at his terraced house in Boston, Lincs, because the back yard is tiny and kitchen waste had 'begun to smell'.

Officials accused him of fly-tipping and issued a £75 fixed penalty – a sum three-quarters his weekly pension – claiming he had filled up the bin unnecessarily.

'I just can't believe this has happened,' he said. 'I've been fined for putting my rubbish in a bin, and that's just ludicrous. The council said I was fly-tipping but I've never thrown litter in my life and brought my children up not to throw litter. I've always put it in a bin.'

Mr Richards learned of his fine when a letter from Boston Borough Council dropped on his doormat. He was warned that if he didn't pay in 14 days the penalty would double and he could face a fine of up to £2,500 in court with jail for non-payment.

Ironically, Mr Richards was fined just days after the council launched a campaign urging the public to make more use of litter bins.

Don't return sand to beach

A PENSIONER who lives beside the seaside has been warned by his council that he faces a heavy fine for fly-tipping if he returns windblown sand in his garden back to the beach.

Arthur Bulmer, 79, has long complained of sand drifting on to his property on the fore-shore at Lytham St Anne's in Lancashire but gales exacerbated the problem.

When he asked Fylde Borough Council if it was permissible to return the sand where it came from, he was told it would constitute fly-tipping. He should treat it as litter and take it to the municipal refuse tip.

The council told him that they willingly clear sand deposited on the public highway but once it lands on private property it becomes the responsibility of the owner.

The pensioner says he now has no alternative but to pay a specialist waste disposal firm to collect the unwanted sand and take it away.

Licence to print money

LITTER wardens in Peterborough working for a private company receive £35 'commission' for every fine they hand out.

Peterborough City Council admitted handing out littering fines to 1,772 pedestrians in 2007, bringing a total of £62,020 in commission.

Police and community support officers can issue the tickets but the vast majority are understood to have been handed out by just two 'environmental wardens' who potentially earned £30,000 each, in addition to their salary of £300 a week.

'Local authorities are already hitting people year after year with above-inflation council tax increases,' says Christine Melsom of the council tax pressure group Is It Fair?

'Now they are giving litter wardens a licence to print money. The scheme encourages wardens to fine people on the flimsiest evidence.'

Councils were given the power to issue fixed-penalty notices under the Clean Neighbourhood and Environment Act 2005.

Bin raiders

CUSTOMERS shopping for clothes at boutique in north London were amazed when two uniformed men marched in and threatened staff with criminal prosecution. They had put their rubbish in the wrong-coloured bin bags.

Council officers announced that the shop in Muswell Hill would be fined £300 after using black bags because they had run out of the grey version issued by the local authority.

The designer store had been waiting more than two weeks for a delivery of new bags but eventually decided to put their rotting rubbish in four standard black bags – a decision which cost them £75 per bag.

'The shop was really busy and they came in here like the Gestapo,' said owner Sangita Ibrahim. 'Staff were told they would face criminal prosecution and receive a criminal record for the bags. I felt like I was going to be frogmarched away.'

Manager Dora Panagi, added: 'Muswell Hill has a real pest

problem and we had food in the bags in the stock room. It started to smell terrible so we put it in four black bags and put two of the grey council bags on top so that they would know it was our rubbish and take it.

'When I came in the next day there was rubbish all over the pavement and I thought that foxes had got to it,' she said. 'Then in walked these two guys looking like policemen with all the badges and the way they dealt with it was horrific.

'One said there had been a criminal offence and I didn't know what he was talking about. My knees were shaking.'

Of course it's hygienic

WITH fortnightly bin collections fast becoming the norm a corresponding risk to public health might be expected. But ministers have tried to keep the wraps on an official report proving just that.

The report found that ending weekly collections would 'significantly alter the pest infestation rates and hence the disease transmission at source', while vermin and insects could be 'encouraged into the home environment'.

But the government held back the £27,000 study by the Central Science Laboratory. Ministers were only forced to release it when the Conservatives tabled a series of Parliamentary questions.

In June 2007, Ben Bradshaw, then an environment minister, claimed there was 'no evidence in published studies' to indicate a link between cutting collections and increased risks to health.

However, Eric Pickles, the shadow local government minister, insists there is a clear health risk from cuts to weekly rubbish collections.

'Under Gordon Brown, local residents are paying exorbitant levels of council tax but are failing to get decent public services in return,' he said. 'People genuinely want to improve recycling and go green, but Labour's approach of forcing rubbish cuts is not the answer, as it will harm the local environment and public health.'

Government figures show that 169 councils out of 350 across England have now ended weekly bin collections. Official guidance from the government quango, Wrap, explains how town halls can end weekly collections and overcome 'public resistance'.

It advised the cuts should be done after local elections to stop people voting against them, and in the autumn or winter so that residents would not immediately notice the extra smells and vermin.

Bin boost for rats

THE end of weekly bin collections has contributed to the dramatic rise in Britain's rat population. According to Rentokil there are 65 to 80 million rats in the UK compared to around 60 million humans.

'In 30 years I've never known such a big rat population,' says Peter Crowden of the National Pest Technicians Association. 'Fortnightly bin collections now mean it's vital we recycle.'

York has more rats than any other city with the population having risen by 208 percent in 2008. Carlisle has seen its rodent population rise by 142 percent, Exeter by 60 percent and Salford by 40 percent.

Nationwide, call-outs by pest control units rose by 17 percent. Out of 50 local authorities asked if they had seen an increase in call-outs, 39 admitted they had.

End of obligation

A LAW dating back 130 years – making it a statutory duty of local authorities to collect household waste – has quietly been done away with. The new rules were introduced without any Parliamentary debate.

Now there are fears that the changes will lead to large increases in fly-tipping, bonfires of noxious substances and rat infestations around uncollected waste. Despite this, there will be no reduction in council tax for home owners.

Phil Woolas, the environment minister, quietly added an amendment to section 46 of the Environmental Protection Act 1990 in July 2008 which now states: 'A waste collection authority is not obliged to collect household waste that is placed for collection in contravention of a requirement under this section.'

Town halls are now free to set their own rules on what constitutes a 'contravention'. Councils could refuse to empty bins that are too far from a curb, are not placed directly outside a gate or are put out on the street too early.

The changes amount to a reversal of the basic right of all households to have their rubbish collected, which was enshrined in law by the Public Health Act 1875.

Binning collections

COUNCILS around Britain are watching a pilot scheme by Brighton and Hove City Council that will see the end of household waste collections altogether. Instead, giant communal bins will be shared among around 40 homes.

The council believes it can save £970,000 over seven years. Already, 500 of the 3,200-litre communal bins have been placed on Brighton's streets, leaving 27,000 families without any form of refuse collection. They are now expected to drag their rubbish up to 150 yards from their home.

Communal bins are already in use for blocks of flats and in some inner-city areas but campaigners believe the Brighton scheme will prove popular with local authorities around the country.

One rule for us

COUNCILS that lay down strict recycling rules on residents often have no idea where the rubbish goes after collection. Millions of tons of waste carefully sorted by householders under fear of harsh fines are regularly dumped in landfills.

The Local Government Association (LGA) admits councils not only have little idea where the rubbish goes but that they are powerless to force private contractors to tell them.

When LGA officials canvassed councils across England and Wales on the tricky question of what happens to the waste, 135 councils failed to respond while 20 said they did not know. A number of council contractors have been caught red-handed dumping the carefully sorted material into landfill sites while others send waste to the Third World.

Much else is stored in vast warehouses now the overseas market for our household waste is drying up.

Only 200 councils claim to know where it all goes. Official figures show that just 34 percent of rubbish is earmarked for recycling but do not show figures for the actual amount recycled.

The LGA's head, Paul Bettison, has appealed to the Environment Agency for new rules to compel contractors to disclose the destination of waste.

THE PATH OF LEAST RESISTANCE

'Anti-social behaviour was becoming a very serious problem on some estates but the courts were too cumbersome a process to deal with it expeditiously. The system was failing' – Tony Blair.

DERMOT Lineham coordinates Croydon's £1.3 million anti-social behaviour 'initiative' with 29 Neighbourhood Enforcement Officers.

So worried was he that they might come to harm while issuing on-the-spot fines for minor offences that he advised them to steer clear of anyone who looked threatening. He advised them to target ordinary people instead.

A clearer explanation of the government's anti-crime policy would be hard to find. In an email to his force, Lineham was emphatic that they focus 'on adults who are less likely to attack us and more likely to pay fixed penalty notices'.

Four legs good, 48 bad

TARA Hewitt has helped fill the government's quotas. She was handed a fixed penalty notice after being caught with four small dogs while waiting for a friend to come and help walk them.

The by-law introduced by Kensington and Chelsea council also limits the length of dog leads to under 4ft. Anyone breaking the order can be issued with an £80 on-the-spot fine.

The local MP, Conservative Sir Malcolm Rifkind, has been swamped with complaints from dog owners but is powerless to intervene. 'As a dog owner I know some people have a legitimate need for a dog-walker because their pets need exercise,' he points out.

A council spokesperson who admitted a certain over-zealousness by his staff, stood his ground, insisting that some cases did warrant action.

'There's a growing concern about some dog-walkers taking as many as 12 dogs out at the same time. In such numbers, dogs are excitable, display pack behaviour and are more than a single walker can handle,' he warned.

'I had no idea about the law but they still gave me a ticket,' said Tara. 'They suggested that if I tried to take it to court I wouldn't have a leg to stand on and I would end up with a bigger fine – up to £1,000.'

Fine for being knocked down

WHEN a police car swerved off the road and ran over Daniel Horne's foot he thought he was owed an apology. But instead he was landed with an £80 fine – for denting the car.

Mr Horne, 28, said he was 'speechless' when the PC who had been at the wheel wrote in the fine notice: 'You ran into the nearside front wing of a marked police vehicle causing a dent.'

The businessman was on his way home from a night out with friends when he was rammed from behind, knocked over and had his foot crushed under the wheel of the patrol car.

Mr Horne said: 'I was in agony with my foot broken in bits and I end up being fined for my body damaging the police car.'

Doctors told Mr Horne of Llanharry, Glamorgan, that he will need to wear a cast for nine weeks.

A South Wales Police spokesperson confirmed that a fixed penalty was issued for criminal damage, adding: 'We have received a complaint from Mr Horne and are looking into it.'

Balloon litter

TEENAGER Max Twizel who let go of a helium balloon at a charity event in Newcastle has been given a £50 fine for littering.

'Will the council fine every charity that holds a balloon race £50 per balloon?' asked his mother. 'How about toddlers in prams who accidentally release their helium balloon?'

However, Stephen Savage, director of regulatory services and public protection at Newcastle Council, said: 'To some people this may sound harsh but we believe that to create a cleaner, safer city we must send out a clear message that this will not be tolerated.'

Crisps cost a packet

BARBARA Jubb was handed an £80 litter fine after her grand-daughter, two-year-old Emily, dropped two crisps on the pavement.

Barbara picked up the bag of Quavers but kicked two stray crisps into the gutter – and was given an on-the-spot fine by two council wardens.

'I was absolutely gobsmacked,' she said. 'I thought Jeremy

Beadle was going to pop out – it was that stupid. People at the bus stop couldn't believe what was going on.'

Crawley Borough Council said it made no apology for targeting people making a mess of its streets. 'People have a responsibility not to drop litter,' said Councillor Beryl Mecrow.

CUT-PRICE COPS

'Want to give something back to your community? Then have you considered taking up a challenging role as a police community support officer?' – police recruitment website.

A RETIRED plumber with a heart condition found himself challenged by a police community support officer while running a few errands for his disabled wife. He would spend the next 18 hours in a police cell and be taken to court in handcuffs. He would also be fingerprinted and have his DNA placed on the National Identity Register

Keith Hirst, 54, was accused of dropping an apple core on the pavement.

After visiting the Post Office near his home in Swinton, Greater Manchester, Keith was heading for the chemists to collect his wife's prescription when a police community support officer (PCSO) accused him of littering.

'There was a chap there in a fluorescent jacket, big sunglasses, and a baseball cap, on a bike, with a wad of tickets and a pen. He said: "Why did you drop that apple core?" and I told him I didn't drop an apple core.'

The officer wanted to issue Keith with a £50 on-the-spot fine for littering.

'He then said he wanted my name and address. He was an over-zealous young lad, baying to give me a ticket. I told him I was on my way to the shops but would be walking back that way if he wanted to speak to me later.'

But when he emerged from the chemists, Keith was suddenly surrounded by five uniformed officers. 'I said I had done nothing wrong and so was not telling them who I was,' Keith told the *Daily Mail.*

He was not allowed to call his family until late that night, during which time he was twice visited in his cell by a doctor after suffering dizzy spells and chest pains.

'The first I knew about it was when Keith called at 10.45pm,' said his wife. 'He'd gone to the Post Office at lunchtime. We didn't know where he was and my daughter had been ringing hospitals.'

A police source upgraded the event for reporters, telling them that Keith had flung the apple core across the road, almost hitting someone. He said regular police officers were called in to back up the PCSO when the accused behaved rudely and aggressively.

But Keith, who vehemently denied all charges, said: 'The way I was treated, you would have thought I had robbed a bank. My family are law-abiding people. This kind of incident does not help in improving relations between the community and police.'

The new force has come in for wide criticism with accusations that the government is saving money by replacing full-time police officers with PCSOs, who cost £10,000 a year less. They were introduced by Home Secretary David Blunkett in 2003 to provide a visible police presence on the street but critics say the PCSOs are a deliberate attempt at misleading the public into believing they have additional protection.

In 2004, their powers were extended under a plan known as *Modernising Police Powers to Meet Community Needs.* At that time, a Home Office spokesperson said it was nonsense to suggest this would mean people facing arrest for littering if they dropped a crisp packet.

Britain now has around 16,000 of the so-called 'plastic policemen', some as young as sixteen.

When Thames Valley Police hired two 16-year-olds, concerns

were raised over public safety. Although too young to watch 18 certificate films, drink in a pub or vote, they have the power to stop and search people under the new terror laws and issue penalty notices for disorder and littering, as well as searching for weapons.

Critics say the 16-year-olds do not have the skills to cope with the demands of front-line policing.

Jan Berry, chairman of the Police Federation, said: 'It puts pressure on them as they neither have the maturity or experience to deal with situations they are likely to confront. This means they are more likely to let down their colleagues and the public.'

Concerns over their lack of training were highlighted after two PCSOs were commended for locking themselves in a room rather than confront an aggressive 13-year-old schoolboy.

Assistant Chief Constable of Devon and Cornwall Police, Sharon Taylor, said: 'Personal safety was their primary concern and they did the right thing. We don't intentionally put them into situations to deal with violent confrontation issues because they are not trained to deal with them.'

This was underlined when two other PCSOs were accused of hiding behind a tree rather than intervene when a gang of teenage girls beat up a man in a Surrey park.

Great-grandmother Ann Ward, 59, who watched the officers dart behind the tree, said: 'It was disgusting – any other men would have stepped in to help.'

She spotted the girls kicking and punching the 55-year-old man in Ravensbury Park near Morden. Mrs Ward said the PCSOs radioed for help but did not tackle them.

'They said they were there to report the crime to the police and take notes,' she said.

In one widely reported incident, police again defended two support officers who stood by and watched while a 10-year-old boy drowned in a pond in Wigan, Greater Manchester. Jordon Lyon died after trying to save his eight-year-old stepsister Bethany.

The inquest into his death heard the PCSOs did not rescue

him as they were not trained to deal with the incident.

His stepfather, Anthony Ganderton, told the inquest: 'I don't know why they didn't go in. I can't understand it. If you see a child drowning you automatically go in that water. You don't care if you're going to lose your job or not. You don't care, do you?'

He also questioned why the PCSOs were unavailable to offer any evidence at the inquest. 'I want to know why they weren't at the inquest when I had to turn up there, and go through the pain of it all. I want to know why they didn't have to be there as main witnesses.'

In a statement, Detective Chief Inspector Phil Owen of Wigan CID, who led the investigation into Jordon's death, said: 'PCSOs are not trained to deal with major incidents such as this. It would have been inappropriate for PCSOs, who are not trained in water rescue, to enter the pond.'

The Police Federation, which represents the interests of regular police officers, has been highly critical of cut-price policing. Manchester regional chairman Paul Kelly said: 'The message is clear and unambiguous – it's the government, they are trying to fool the public. They take a person and dress him up as a police officer but they just don't have the same powers.'

This is a point lost on the union, Unison, which represents around 6,000 PCSOs on the beat in England and Wales. One way of improving the standing of their members, they claim, would be to give them the same uniforms as ordinary police officers.

The union has designed a uniform which is almost identical to that of a regular police officer, except the tie and epaulettes are blue rather than black.

It is calling for a more standard uniform and standard equipment, including stab vests, for all community officers so the public do not confuse them with parking attendants.

But Jan Berry of the Police Federation said Unison's suggestion would serve 'no greater purpose than fooling the public into thinking there are more officers on the beat than in reality there are'.

Street crime

TWO PCSOs were quick to act when a neighbour complained that children were playing traditional games in the street.

Kayleigh Mangan and Georgina Smallwood, both 14, had chalked four or five hopscotch grids on the pavement in Spring Street, Stourbridge, outside their homes.

They were mortified when police community support officers called on Kayleigh's mum, Lisa, and said they had received a complaint. They then made the girls scrub all but one of the grids off the pavement.

Ironically, a local Neighbourhood Watch newsletter had earlier suggested children play traditional games like spinning tops and hopscotch after police sent round letters telling kids not to play ball games.

According to Mrs Mangan, the PCSOs were kicking up a storm over nothing. 'It's not spray paint, it was supposed to rain which would have washed them off. It was amazing how quickly they responded to something so trivial.'

A spokesperson for West Midlands Police said they were forced to intervene before more serious crimes were committed.

'We received a complaint regarding numerous chalk markings on a large stretch of the pavement,' she said. 'There have been many reports of anti-social behaviour in the area and we will deal robustly with this issue.

'We will continue to respond positively to community complaints and concerns to combat fear of crime.'

Preaching hate

A POLICE community support officer stepped in to prevent two Christian preachers from handing out Bible tracts in a Muslim area, saying attempting to convert Muslims to Christianity was a hate crime.

The preachers, Americans Arthur Cunningham and Joseph Abraham, say their treatment breaks the Human Rights Act, which guarantees freedom of religious expression.

Mr Abraham, 65, who was born a Muslim in Egypt and is a convert to Christianity, said: 'He told us we were trying to convert Muslims to Christianity and that that was a hate crime. He was very intimidating and it concerns me that somebody holding his views can become a police officer, albeit at PCSO level.'

According to Mr Cunningham, 48, a fellow Baptist missionary: 'He said we were in a Muslim area and were not allowed to spread our Christian message. He said he was going to take us to the police station.'

CASH COWS ON WHEELS

'I believe in policies that support road safety and the motorist. Cars support our economy' – Stephen Ladyman, Minister of State for Transport [2005-2007].

ALMOST half of all criminal cases punished by the courts are for minor motoring offences while the number of serious crimes dealt with by judges and magistrates such as violent attacks are on the decrease.

RAC Foundation spokesman Kevin Delaney, former head of traffic policing with the Metropolitan Police, says there is one law for motorists and another for hardened criminals.

'If burglars, thieves and anti-social yobs were tackled by the police with the same enthusiasm and zero tolerance as motorists, drivers would understand,' he maintains.

'The problem is that most motorists are law-abiding and that makes them a soft target. Unlike hardened criminals, they tend not to bash the copper who stops them for speeding.'

Marc McArthur-Christie of the Association of British Drivers believes: 'The government has declared war on the motorist while declaring surrender on serious crime.'

Local authorities collected more than £173 million in Penalty Charge Notices in 2007, up £12.5 million on the year before – a rise of 7.7 percent.

Campaigners described the amount collected as an 'excessive and unfair' imposition on already hard-pressed drivers, adding that motorists are being unfairly punished for the shortage of parking spaces in many towns and cities.

When it comes to taxes, UK motorists are now paying in excess of £143 million a day in road user taxes. For every £100 a motorist spends on fuel, between £60 and £70 is duty and VAT which means that in one year the government makes around £900 from the average driver on tax and duties alone.

And it doesn't have to be legal

COUNCILS are raking in tens of millions of pounds by enforcing unlawful traffic and parking restrictions, says Oliver Mishcon, a barrister who specialises in motoring cases.

Fines are being levied on innocent motorists by councils accused of a host of abuses including incorrect road markings and parking bays which are too small.

Up to seven out of ten fines are thrown out on appeal if motorists can be bothered to contest them. But many are put off because they risk losing their 50 percent discount for early payment.

'It's a massive problem on a national scale and we're talking about councils making tens of millions of pounds,' says Mr Mishcon. 'From a legal point of view, the term is unjust enrichment. And if the council unjustly enriches itself, it's got to pay the money back.'

Alan Stanton, a Labour councillor in the London borough of Haringey, maintains his borough has continued ticketing two yellow box junctions in Tottenham even after they were found to be unlawful.

'We have taken £120,000 from people we had no right to take from,' he explained.

Motorists complain that dodgy practices are taking place throughout Britain. Critics have highlighted problems with the incorrectly-marked entrance to a bus and tram lane which earned Sheffield City Council £350,000.

The London Borough of Camden collected more than £245,000 from motorists who drove down a pedestrian street which had not been clearly signposted.

Nice little earner

A MILLION more speeding tickets are being issued every year than a decade ago, raising £1 billion a year in fines.

David Ruffley, shadow police reform minister, said official figures showed 1,773,412 fixed penalty notices were given to drivers in 2006, up from 712,753 in 1997. These were for motorists caught on camera as well as those stopped by the police.

'Ministers need to tell us what they are doing with this £100 million a year taken from motorists,' said Mr Ruffley.

'How much is actually put back into practical road safety that does not involve speed cameras? Ministers' failure to answer that question confirms the view that for this government the British motorist is a nice little earner.'

Roads worsen

TWO OUT of three AA members think Britain's roads are in a worse state than they were ten years ago. Of the nearly 18,000 members canvassed by the motoring organisation, 40 percent said road surfaces were much worse.

Roads in Yorkshire and the Humber region got the worst ratings from the survey and Northern Ireland the best.

AA president Edmund King says motorists receive poor value for money for the tax they pay. 'These findings come as a stark reminder that, despite some extra government funding for road maintenance at the start of the decade, the cash is nowhere enough for drivers to see real improvement in road conditions.'

'Skimping on maintenance can cost lives and not a single one should be lost on the roads for want of a pothole being filled or surface renewed.'

Parking profit

THE COST of leaving your car in a council-run car park has risen by 14 percent in just two years, according to figures released by the Department of Communities and Local Government.

Charges for off-street parking brought town halls just over £554 million in 2005. That rose to £599 million in 2006 and £633 million in 2007. Figures for 2008-2009 are expected to show a further increase.

Among those authorities that managed big increases in their profits was Bournemouth, with receipts up 70 percent to just over £10 million; Kennet, where a 453 percent rise pushed takings to over £1 million; and Reigate and Banstead, which showed a 480 percent increase with receipts of just under £1.6 million. Tameside increased its car park takings by 3,267 percent to £1.75 million.

CCTV safer for attendants

CCTV cameras are now being used to issue parking fines, reducing the risk of assault on the tens of thousands of parking attendants – now renamed 'civil enforcement officers'.

Drivers will not know that they have been caught until a letter arrives up to 14 days later, by which time they may be unable to gather evidence to defend themselves.

Cameras are being employed in areas where it is too 'difficult or sensitive' for an attendant to operate.

Ministers say the changes make parking enforcement 'fairer and more transparent', although the AA insists that thousands of innocent drivers will receive penalties from attendants seeking an easy way to meet performance targets.

Finger of fate

A MOTORIST has been fined £80 for giving a speed camera the finger.

Simon Thompson, 41, made the middle finger curse when he spotted the mobile camera as he drove home from work *within* the speed limit.

He was stunned half an hour later when two policemen knocked on his door and handed him a fixed penalty notice for making offensive gestures under the Public Order Act.

Size matters

PARKING charges are now being introduced based on the length of the car. Norwich City Council is the first local authority to implement the controversial measure which penalises owners of vehicles over 14½ feet in length, such as the Vauxhall Vectra.

Brian Morrey, vice-chairman of the Norwich Highways Agency Committee, said: 'We want to encourage more people to drive smaller cars. It is far more environmentally friendly and would also generate more parking space on the roads.'

However, motoring organisations say the move is meaningless as it fails to discriminate between eco-friendly cars and gas-guzzlers.

'What if you drive a Toyota Prius, which is quite a big car but has very low emissions, or a large electric vehicle?' asked NCP, the traffic enforcement company. 'Would you have to pay more too?'

Under the terms of the scheme, drivers of outsized cars would pay an annual parking charge of £30, nearly double their current tariff of £16.

A spokesperson for the RAC Foundation said: 'This new system will discriminate against families with children, who are more likely to drive longer vehicles like estate cars.'

A spokesperson for the Local Government Association said: 'Councils will be watching with great interest to see how well this scheme works. Councils will continue to pilot schemes that improve air quality in city centres and help to tackle pollution.'

Fine for over-payment

AIMEE GREEN did not have change when she parked in the Lion Green car park in Coulsdon so she paid £1 for her 80p ticket. Nor surprisingly, she was horrified to discover 15 minutes later that a traffic warden had given her a parking ticket.

The 'enforcement officer' claimed she had parked illegally – because she did not put exactly 80p in the machine.

Miss Green from Purley said: 'I tried to explain to him that I didn't have any change, but he just kept saying, 'Look at the sign, it says 80p. You put in £1, look at the sign.'

She told the *Croydon Advertiser*: 'Parking in Lion Green car park is clearly a minefield where parking attendants feel they can issue tickets based on the most obscure and incomprehensible reasons.'

Croydon Council eventually cancelled the fine on appeal and a spokesperson said: 'The parking attendant involved has been spoken to and warned his future performance will be closely monitored to ensure he is fully aware of the council's service delivery expectations.'

Timed out

THE inability to tell the time led a Torquay traffic warden to issue an innocent motorist with a parking ticket. He used a calculator to work out the expiry time of Dave Alsop's ticket without realising the device worked in decimals and not minutes and hours.

Mr Alsop, 29, parked near Torquay harbour, Devon, at 2.49pm

and paid £1.20 for 75 minutes, covering him until 4.04pm. But when he returned at 3.41pm, he discovered a £50 fine on his car.

He found the warden and showed him the parking ticket, which clearly had time left on it. The warden disagreed and tried to prove his point with a calculator.

'I tried to explain but he didn't have a clue,' said Mr Alsop. 'He just carried on doing other cars parked there.'

Torbay council waived the fee and apologised, saying the 'civil enforcement officer' was new on the job.

No need for signs

DRIVERS who park 'inconsiderately' could be fined £70 under a new ruling that eliminates the need for warning signs or road-markings.

The AA has condemned the move as 'unfair' and 'very dodgy', saying drivers could unwittingly incur a parking fine with no chance of a successful appeal.

Councils now have new powers to issue tickets to drivers who park more than 18in from the pavement – called double-parking – or who block driveways or obstruct pavements lowered for wheelchairs or prams.

The changes mean that drivers can be prosecuted even if there is no sign or road marking alerting them to any potential offence.

Three strikes and clamp

MOTORISTS in London who fail to pay three parking tickets face having their cars clamped or towed away under strict new rules.

'Civil enforcement officers' with hand-held computers can now access a register of persistent parking offenders.

If they spot a car's unpaid penalties they can call in the clampers or tow it away until the cash is recovered.

Motorists who fail to pay fines for other offences, such as

driving in a bus lane or blocking a yellow box junction, face a similar punishment.

Other councils across the country are watching closely. The four London authorities holding a six-month trial of the new powers are Ealing, Hammersmith and Fulham, Kensington & Chelsea, and Transport for London, the body responsible for all the main roads across the capital.

However, Barrie Segal of motorists' champion Appeal Now fears innocent motorists could run foul of the crackdown.

'There is a danger that cars will be towed away to the obscurity of a car pound when appeals are pending,' he warned. 'This is going to put enormous burdens on a motorist in making sure that councils have registered an appeal.'

The government had originally floated the idea of a national 'three tickets and you're clamped' system but got cold feet in the wake of a series of database blunders.

Now it says it is up to local authorities to organise themselves if they want to share data.

Taxing space

DRIVING to work will become even more expensive with the introduction of a controversial scheme to tax employers who provide more than 10 parking spaces.

Under the Workplace Parking Levy, all businesses with company parking must apply for a licence whether they qualify for the charge or not. The new rules – to be introduced in 2010 – will be enforced by CCTV cameras, spot checks and number plate registration systems.

Paul Southby of the Confederation of British Industry says it will do nothing to tackle road congestion. 'As far as we are concerned, it placcs businesses hit by the levy at an unfair advantage, locally, nationally and internationally.'

Nottingham Council hopes to be the first to introduce the scheme. Council leader Jon Collins says councils must tackle the menace of growing road use. 'Any city that does not plan to meet these challenges is not planning ahead for sustainable growth. Future generations will thank us,' he says.

Nottingham business leader George Cowcher is not convinced. 'Cutting through the rhetoric, it's a tax on jobs and competitiveness, which is unpopular both with businesses and workers alike, and comes at a time when we are seeing the worst trading conditions in decades.'

No hiding place

A NEW generation of speed cameras will make it impossible to evade detection by monitoring motorists' average speed during their journey. The Spec3 cameras which never run out of film are expected to be deployed in their hundreds with the first fines issued by summer 2009.

The cameras, which work in networks of 50 devices, can each be positioned more than 15 miles apart and automatically read number plates. Data is transmitted instantly to a penalty processing centre.

Road Safety Minister Jim Fitzpatrick insists the cameras will benefit road users. 'I think there will be great interest among the safety-camera partnerships,' he says. 'They will give a more sophisticated edge to cameras than the blunt instrument we have at the moment.'

Cops get all journey details

LEAKED Whitehall documents have revealed plans to hand the police details of the daily journeys of millions of motorists tracked by road pricing cameras across the country.

The Home Office says the police need the data from the cameras, which can read and store every passing number plate, 'for all crime fighting purposes'.

There are already nearly 2,000 automatic number plate

recognition cameras in place and they are due to double as road pricing schemes are expanded across the country.

The leaked Home Office note emerged as it was announced that the then Home Secretary Jacqui Smith had waived Data Protection Act safeguards to allow the bulk transfer of data from London's congestion charge and traffic cameras to the Metropolitan Police for the specific purpose of tracking potential terrorists in and around the capital.

Shami Chakrabarti, the director of Liberty, said: 'It is one thing to ask the public for special measures to fight the grave threat of terrorism, but when that becomes a Trojan horse for mass snooping for more petty matters it only leads to a loss of trust in government.'

WASTING POLICE TIME

The police want to reduce public fear of crime and do more to build public confidence. This is being done through the police reform programme and reforms to the criminal justice system' – Home Office website.

THE middle classes have lost all confidence in the police says the Civitas think-tank because they routinely target ordinary people rather than actual criminals to fill government crime quotas. The attitude of some officers has also led to spiralling complaints about neglect of duty and rudeness.

The report warns that a generation of young people – 'the police's favourite soft targets' – are being criminalised, putting their future prospects at risk.

The report's author, Harriet Sergeant, says: 'The police cannot police without the backing of society. Without trust and consensus, it is very difficult and costly to maintain law and order.'

Her report says: 'Complaints against the police have risen, with much of the increase coming from law-abiding, middle-class, middle-aged and retired people who no longer feel the police are on their side.'

The report details how officers are expected to reach a certain number of 'sanction detections' a month by charging, cautioning or fining 'offenders'.

Arresting or fining someone for a trifling offence – such as a child stealing a Mars bar – is a good way of hitting the target and pleasing the Home Office, and scores as highly as catching a killer, she explained.

Hate mail

A TEN-year-old boy was reduced to tears when police arrived at his home to investigate allegations of a homosexual hate crime after he allegedly called a school friend 'gay' in an email.

His father, Alan Rawlinson, said he was astounded when two officers arrived at his home in Bold Heath, Cheshire. 'I could not believe what I was hearing,' he said. 'They told me they considered it a very serious offence. I thought they were joking.'

Mr Rawlinson runs a construction company and deals with problems of theft on a regular basis. His wife is a magistrate who sees serious crimes all the time.

'This just seemed a huge waste of resources for something so trivial,' he said. 'I am furious about what has happened, it just seems the politically correct brigade are taking over.'

He said his son, George, a pupil at Farnworth primary school in Widnes, was terrified when police arrived. 'My son is not anti anybody, he is too young to have made judgments about people and we have always taught him to judge people as he finds them.'

'There is no evidence he sent this email, but even if he did I'm sure the words have been taken the wrong way. If somebody had called the police about something like this in my day they would have laughed.'

Inspector Nick Bailey, of Cheshire Constabulary, said: 'Going to the boy's house was a reasonable course of action to take. The use of the word "gay" would imply this is homophobic, but we would be hard-pushed to say this is a homophobic crime.'

Granny ball theft

A DERBYSHIRE grandmother was arrested after being accused of stealing a football which she says landed in her back garden.

Angela Hickling, 56, from Heanor, was arrested on suspicion of theft over the lost ball after neighbours reported her to police, claiming their sons had kicked the ball into her garden and she refused to return it.

Mother-of-three Mrs Hickling explained to police when they arrived at her home that she had looked for the ball but could not find it.

Officers then searched her home and she was then taken into custody where she was interviewed and had her fingerprints and DNA taken.

'It was just incredible. I was taken in an unmarked police car to the divisional headquarters, subject to a photograph with a number on it, DNA, fingerprinting, everything.'

Gay horse slur leads to arrest

POLICE officers who arrested a student for calling a police horse 'gay' have been accused of 'absurd heavy-handedness and over-reaction' by a leading campaigner for homosexual rights.

Peter Tatchell of the pressure group Outrage! said the arrest of Sam Brown 'brought the police service into disrepute'.

Mr Brown, 21, a student at Oxford's Balliol College, was arrested for causing harassment, alarm or distress and fined £80 after asking a mounted police officer if he knew that his horse was homosexual.

The student made the remark during a night out in Oxford

where he was celebrating completing his English Literature degree.

Mr Tatchell accused the police of grossly wasting their time and resources. 'The police are not doing nearly enough to halt genuine violence against gay people and yet they waste their time on this absurd arrest,' he said.

The undergraduate had approached two mounted policemen in the city centre after leaving a bar where he had been drinking with friends. He was then handcuffed and taken to a police station where he was given a fixed penalty notice after spending the night in a cell.

'The whole thing is absolutely absurd,' said Mr Brown. 'There were about six police officers and a whole load of patrol cars.'

TV man hunt

POLICE in Belfast launched a high-profile manhunt lasting six hours when a man fled custody after failing to find enough money to pay a TV license fine.

Leon Chakravarti, 21, said he panicked and fled when he realised he did not have enough cash to pay the £182.60 fine.

'Apparently, the demands for money had been sent to my old address. It was the first I knew about it,' he explained.

He said his job was put on the line and many people think he is a hardened criminal. 'My life is so messed up because of a stupid £180 fine that I knew nothing about,' he said.

'The police should be out getting proper criminals, like those people out stealing, burgling houses, torturing elderly people. All I did was not pay a fine which I knew absolutely nothing about.'

Wrap for playground push

POLICE stormed into a school to arrest a 14-year-old boy for pushing over a fellow classmate in the playground who he suspected of bullying his younger brother.

The boy, a prefect described as a 'model pupil', was given a formal reprimand by officers after an investigation. His name and offence have been placed on the Police National Computer.

His reprimand for a 'violent crime' will also remain on the separate Criminal Record Bureau (CRB) database, jeopardising his hopes of following in his parents' footsteps and becoming a teacher.

The police action was condemned by local MP Grant Shapps. 'Parents will be concerned to hear police are invading the classroom rather than solving violent street crime,' he said.

'I fear this is the government's target culture gone mad. Officers are meeting their targets for solving violent crime by busying themselves in the playground and undermining the authority of schools in the process.'

The incident was the result of an alleged six-month racist bullying campaign against the boy's 11-year-old brother after he started at the same secondary school in Welwyn Garden City, Herts.

The boy finally decided to confront one of the alleged tormentors who then told a teacher he had been pushed over.

The boy's father, Guya Persaud, 50, is a deputy head teacher at a London school. His wife Sorel, 48, is also a teacher.

'It will show up on criminal record bureau checks for the rest of his life,' he said. 'As a deputy head, I know that if a school gets a positive CRB check on an application from someone to be a teacher, it goes straight to the bottom of the pile.'

Arrest over nursery tiff

NURSERY owner Olive Rack, 55, was charged with common assault after intervening to stop a toddler hitting a baby with a wooden brick.

The offence was brought to police notice by two Northamptonshire county council officials who were visiting the nursery to advise on funding.

Although the toddler's parents made no complaint and continued to send their little girl to the nursery, Mrs Rack was charged with assaulting the two-and-a-half year old when she took her by the arm, sat her on a chair and told her off for striking a 12-month-old baby with a toy brick.

Mrs Rack, a qualified nursery nurse who has run nurseries for 19 years, said she had followed standard procedures and denied any suggestion of assault.

'I was talking to two council workers, who had their back to the play area, when I saw a little girl pick up a large toy brick and hit the baby over the head,' she said. 'She was about to do it again when I rushed into the room to stop her.'

Mrs Rack insists that her actions were no different to those taken by parents and childcare workers in similar circumstances.

'There was nothing unusual in the way I dealt with it,' she said. 'It was an everyday thing and I thought no more about it.'

A spokesperson for Northamptonshire police said that Mrs Rack had been charged with common assault following the incident.

A number of recent cases have seen teachers prosecuted or facing the sack because of attempts to discipline children.

Ian Mackay, 55, the head teacher of Scotby Church of England School near Carlisle was suspended after he pulled two boys out of the way to free a 10-year-old girl they had trapped in a dark storeroom. The parents of one boy claimed that he bruised their son's arm.

Norwich magistrates earlier cleared teacher Willem van Trotsenburg of assaulting a disruptive girl he had grabbed by the arm and removed from class. Prosecutors claimed that the head of mathematics had used 'unreasonable' force against the 14-year-old.

And Carron Downer, a PE teacher, was found guilty of assault by North Avon magistrates after grabbing and pushing a pupil who had deliberately barged into him.

Tesco shops hunter

A DEER hunter who took his photographs to a supermarket for processing was shocked to find himself reported to police. Although the sport is legal, Tesco gave his details to officers who questioned him for several hours.

The man, who asked to remain anonymous, said he was 'made to feel like a terrorist'.

Tesco has no ban on photographs of shooting and its privacy policy clearly states: 'We will never pass your personal data to anyone else'.

Simon Hart, the chief executive of the Countryside Alliance, which campaigns on rural issues, said: 'This is one of the most disturbing and ridiculous examples of ignorance and demonisation of which Tesco should be ashamed.'

However, Tesco's chief executive Sir Terry Leahy defended his staff's actions.

'On being asked to view the prints, our store's management team decided that there was cause for concern and as such contacted the police,' he explained.

Boots put gloss on varnish thief

WHEN grammar school girl Hannah Gilbert, 12, popped into Boots on her second ever trip into town by herself she thought nothing of painting a single thumb with nail polish to see how it looked.

But her shopping expedition turned into a nightmare when a security guard told her that if she failed to buy the product she would be guilty of theft.

Tearful Hannah, a member of a Christian youth fellowship group, did not have enough money to pay for the £6.29 peach-coloured Revlon polish so she was detained until police arrived

Mother Cheryl said when she arrived at the store Hannah was scared and crying. 'I find it incredibly hard to believe this was the most serious incident going on for the police to deal with,' she said, adding that she hopes to leave Britain as soon as possible.

'Frankly, this country has gone crazy,' she said.

The police explained that they had the power to forcibly restrain Hannah as she was over the age of ten.

A Boots spokesperson added: 'Mrs Gilbert's daughter remained on the premises until she was able to be released safely into the care of her parents.'

'These safety measures are in place to ensure our customers have a continued safe shopping environment,' he explained.

No debate in race hate

POLICE called to Harrop Fold High School in Worsley arrested a teenage schoolgirl for a race hate crime after she asked not to sit with a group of Asian students during a class debate because only one of them could speak English.

Codie Stott, 14, was forced to spend three-and-a-half hours in a police cell after she was reported by her teachers.

The teenager had not been in school the day before due to a hospital appointment and had missed the start of a project, so the teacher allocated her a group to sit with.

'She said I had to sit there with five Asian pupils,' explained Codie. 'I said I'm not being funny, but can I change groups because I can't understand them?'

Codie insists the teacher then lost her temper and began shouting and screaming, saying: 'It's racist, you're going to get done by the police.'

Later at Swinton police station, Codie was placed under arrest. 'They told me to take my laces out of my shoes and remove my jewellery, and I had my fingerprints and photograph taken,' she said. 'It was awful.'

After questioning on suspicion of committing a section five racial public order offence, her mother Nicola says she was placed in a bare cell for three-and-a-half hours then released without charge.

Headteacher Dr Antony Edkins said: 'An allegation of a serious nature was made concerning a racially motivated remark by one student towards a group of Asian students new to the school and new to the country.'

'We aim to ensure a caring and tolerant attitude towards people and pupils of all ethnic backgrounds and will not stand for racism in any form,' he explained.

Tree House Three nabbed

POLICE locked three children in cells for two hours after they were caught climbing a tree on public land in Halesowen, West Midlands.

The afternoon adventure turned into a frightening ordeal for Sam Cannon, Amy Higgins and Katy Smith after they climbed the 20ft tree – then found themselves hauled into a police station where their shoes were removed, their photos taken and DNA samples swabbed from their mouths.

Questioned by police, the scared friends admitted they had broken some loose branches because they had wanted to build a tree house but said they did not realise what they had done was wrong.

Their parents accused police of over-reacting and treating their children like hardened criminals. Amy's mother, Jacqueline, said her daughter was left so traumatised by the police action that she refused to sleep in her bed for a week.

'Amy was scared bucket-loads to be locked up in a cell knowing murderers and rapists have been sat in the same cells. The police action was completely unbalanced,' she said. 'These were children playing in a tree!'

The information taken by the police will be held permanently on the national database and Amy is worried it could affect her going to college or university.

Sam's father, Nicholas, 52, said: 'The children did not deserve to be treated in this way. Sam's eyes were swollen and red when they let him out of the cell as he had been crying.'

Superintendent Stuart Johnson, operations manager at Halesowen police station, said: 'I support the actions of my officers who responded to complaints from the public about kids destroying an ornamental cherry tree by stripping every branch from it, in an area where there have been reports of anti-social behaviour.'

'West Midlands Police deals robustly with anti-social behaviour. By targeting what may seem relatively low-level crime we aim to prevent it developing into more serious matters.'

WIDENING THE DRAGNET

On-the-spot fines 'reduce the burden on the courts, free police to patrol the streets and ensure those committing minor offences are punished, rather than let off with a warning' – Home Office statement.

THE government is putting 'punishment before justice' with thousands of people consigned to a new class of "semi-criminals" by on-the-spot fines for minor offences says the Crime and Society Foundation – a leading criminal justice think-tank.

The foundation says people who pay 'summary' fines – in the mistaken belief that they are not an admission of guilt – could have their 'admission' used against them in future.

'This risks creating a new 'semi-criminal' class, those with no formal criminal record yet deemed to be offenders,' it says, adding that such fines operating outside the constraints of criminal justice, remove important protections for members of the public.

And it says the fines create a 'two-tier justice system' with the well-off buying their way out of further action, while poorer people have to take their chance in court.

The report says the government has widened the 'criminal

justice dragnet' to bring in more people – particularly children – who might previously have escaped with an informal caution.

'It's a bizarre state of affairs when an individual is required to pay a fine for a crime without going to court and without having to admit guilt,' says Richard Garside, the foundation's director and a co-author of the report

'It's a good wheeze for ministers and the police because it creates the illusion of justice being done and crime being tackled. But penalty notices for disorders are more about extending the reach of the police and the criminal justice system than delivering genuine justice or promoting greater safety.'

Stand and deliver

ON-THE-SPOT fines are being issued at a rate of one every three minutes, a rise of almost 40 percent in a year.

However, police representatives claim that the need to meet the target of bringing 1.25 million offences to justice a year has 'corrupted' the use of on-the-spot fines by encouraging officers to use them inappropriately.

Chief Superintendent Derek Barnett, vice-president of the Police Superintendents' Association, said: 'Policing is often about common sense and resolving difficult circumstances with discretion. But some individual officers are choosing not to use their discretion perhaps because they feel it is a way of fulfilling the government's target.'

Offenders pay either a £50 or £80 penalty even though they may have caused criminal damage of £500 or stolen up to £200 of goods from a shop. Many shopkeepers bitterly oppose the fines, claiming that they encourage shoplifting by effectively letting offenders off.

How to clear the courts

MAGISTRATES are finding that they have a lot more time on

their hands. The use of on-the-spot fines has seen the number of formal criminal court hearings reduced to the point where courts are regularly closed through lack of work.

An internal memo reveals how the use of summary justice is now leaving the courts with very little to do.

'As a result of a reducing workload directly attributable to increased use of fixed penalties and cautions by the police and Crown Prosecution Service, a number of courts have had to be cancelled each week at each of our court houses.'

The memo, from Staffordshire's justices' clerk and seen by *The Times*, goes on to explain that the overall number of courts in the county is to be cut because of falling demand.

'I am deeply concerned about the increased use by the prosecuting agencies of judicial powers but it seems that those powers are likely to be used increasingly given that they are a cheaper means of sentencing than by going through a judicial process,' he said.

According to *The Times*, the number of penalty notices issued for disorder rose by 37 percent from 146,500 in 2005 to 201,200 in 2007. The majority were for behaviour likely to 'cause harassment, alarm or distress' and being drunk and disorderly.

The number issued for shoplifting almost doubled from 23,800 in 2005 to 42,700 in 2006. In Staffordshire, penalty notices for disorder rose from 1,450 in 2004 to 3,261 in 2006.

Magistrates' court proceedings for shoplifting have fallen by 29 percent since 2005, drunkenness by 51 percent and for being drunk and disorderly by 44 percent.

'The increasing use of penalty notices is leading to soft justice, where offenders who should go before the courts are able to escape with a fine which they might not even pay,' says Shadow Justice Secretary Nick Herbert.

On-the-spot fines were introduced to allow police to deal with simple and straightforward cases promptly, leaving courts to handle disputed and more complex offences. But barristers and solicitors complain that fines and cautions are actually being used for the more serious crimes.

'We are extremely concerned if an inappropriate use of out-of-courts disposals is removing serious cases from court,' explained Cindy Barnett, the chairman of the Magistrates' Association.

Mind how you go

POLICE are letting three-times as many violent offenders escape justice today than they were five years ago, with cautions now overtaking convictions as punishment for the first time.

The rapid expansion of 'instant justice' under New Labour has seen a dramatic rise in the use of formal warnings, cautions and on-the-spot fines by police as an alternative to criminal charges, says Professor Rod Morgan, former chairman of the Youth Justice Board.

Professor Morgan's report, published by the Centre for Crime and Justice Studies (CCJS), shows an alarming growth in instant justice and says police and prosecutors have embraced the policy.

Cautions handed out for 'more serious violence against the person' rose by 92 percent to 916 between 2001 and 2006. While convictions also rose, the proportion of offenders charged and sent to court plunged from 63 percent to just 41 percent.

Although the total number of offences brought to justice grew from just over a million in 1999 to 1.4million in 2007, virtually all the increase was accounted for by the rise in cautions, fines and formal warnings.

And Professor Morgan warns that the increase is largely at the expense of previously law abiding citizens. The use of these powers, he says, is 'dragging into the criminal justice system offenders and offending behaviour that would not previously have been criminalised' – particularly 'marginal' offences by young people.

The Department of Justice, however, sees value in the system. 'The law-abiding majority want to see crimes dealt with effectively and fixed penalty notices and cautions are part of this process,' explained a spokesperson.

'Whether this state of affairs corresponds with what most members of the public would consider justice seems at best a moot point,' says the CCJS.

2

NOTHING TO HIDE, NOTHING TO FEAR

'I can't see what all the fuss is about. I always say if you've nothing to hide, you've nothing to fear' – caller to BBC Radio 4's 'Any Answers' programme.

WITH up to eight new laws passed every day how do people know if they have nothing to hide? Ignorance is no excuse in the eyes of the law, so the onus is on the general public to keep abreast of all new legislation – even though the government itself admits it has no idea just how many laws are currently on the statute books.

According to the legal publishers Sweet & Maxwell, 3,071 new laws were passed in 2007, a 14 percent jump on the previous year. And Gordon Brown's record is even worse than that of Tony Blair, with 17 percent more laws in his first 12 months – despite a clear pledge to cut red tape.

'If legislation was a guarantee of greater public safety, this country would be the safest nation on earth,' insists Nick Clegg of the Liberal Democrats.

'This is panic, push-button government at its worst. New laws are produced with the aim of chasing headlines, not pursuing the guilty, whilst the innocent will be harassed by illiberal legislation forced onto the statute book on little more than a ministerial whim,' he says.

With such a tsunami of new laws, the average Briton is committing a crime a day according to on-line pollsters, OnePoll.

Speeding, using a mobile phone while driving and 'eco-crimes' top the list of rules and regulations regularly flouted. Only five percent of Britons say they never break any laws.

Who, for example, knows that it is now illegal to import Polish potatoes or trade in grey squirrels, ruddy ducks and Japanese knotweed? How many householders know they have a legal obligation under the Clean Neighbourhoods and Environment Act 2005 to nominate a key-holder for their burglar alarm every time they go on holiday?

Some of the new laws would appear more than obvious. For example, you can no longer offer air traffic control services without a licence. But, in its second year, New Labour felt the need to ban people from creating their very own nuclear explosions.

Open door policy

A PERSON'S home is no longer their castle but a 'right of way' for police, local government officials and other bureaucrats according to a report from the Centre for Policy Studies.

In the 1950s just 10 new powers of entry were granted by statute. Today, there are around 266 ways says barrister Harry Snook, author of the study *Crossing the Threshold.*

'The State today enjoys widespread access to what was previously considered the private domain. Entry powers – many from the EU – have proliferated over recent decades,' he insists.

One of the most powerful bodies is HM Revenue and Customs whose officers can exercise a 'writ of assistance' with almost unlimited rights of access. They can break into private houses to seize any goods which they believe are liable to be forfeit.

'As a result of the proliferation and variety of entry powers, a citizen cannot realistically be aware of the circumstances in which his home may be entered by State officials without his consent, or what rights he has in such circumstances,' says the report.

'Force can be used in the exercise of almost all these powers. In many cases, discretion as to what is considered 'reasonable behaviour' in gaining entry is left to the judgment of those wielding the entry power.'

But Mr Snook says: 'Many powers are drafted so broadly that the citizen has little or no protection if officials behave officiously or vindictively. Some carry draconian penalties for obstruction, including heavy fines and prison sentences of up to two years.'

If that wasn't enough, an internal Home Office report discovered an additional 813 laws and regulations which permit officials to force entry into homes, cars and business premises, making 1,043 in total.

The dossier, compiled by Security Minister Lord West, details the often obscure acts and regulations which give the authorities the power to break into homes.

Hundreds of new powers of entry have been created since 1997, including ones relating to illegal gambling, congestion charging, high hedges and weapons of mass destruction.

West's report details 753 separate 'big brother' provisions in acts of Parliament and a further 290 minor regulations. A total of 430 of these powers have been approved by Parliament since New Labour came to power.

Watch what you sign

HOUSEHOLDERS are being warned to read their council tax returns carefully or risk opening the door to an army of snoopers.

By failing to agree to a 'spot check', residents will not be able to gain discounts, a move that affects 7.5 million people – many of them pensioners – claiming the single person's allowance.

One form from Thurrock Council in Essex, reads: 'To be completed and returned immediately if you wish to continue to claim single person discount...I authorise the Council or its agents to make enquiries to corroborate this claim. I will permit the Council or its agents to inspect the property on request...'

'If you do not do so,' says the form, 'we will have to cancel your discount and send you a revised bill for the increased amount.'

Shadow local government secretary Eric Pickles warns: 'It may be appropriate for local authorities to check that council tax discounts are not wrongly claimed. But it is wholly disproportionate to threaten higher council tax bills if residents do not allow State officials into their bedrooms. This is another worrying sign of function creep.'

Tax doesn't have to be threatening

TAX inspectors now have wide-ranging powers to bug people's homes and private phone calls. They can also intercept emails and plant listening devices in suspects' cars and offices.

Previously, revenue officers worked with strict safeguards that even banned them from looking in cupboards. Now they can pry into every aspect of a suspect's life in the hunt for evidence.

The new laws were introduced as part of legislation to tackle organised crime and gun-running, and give HMCR parity in the use of surveillance with MI5, GCHQ and the police.

The Institute of Chartered Accountants considers the new powers to be excessive. 'There is no evidence that bugging is needed in relation to tax fraud,' insists spokesman Harry Travers:

'Inspectors already have wide-ranging powers to obtain search warrants, raid people's property, seize documents and computers. They don't need to be able to bug people as well. There is real risk of breaching human rights.'

Coming through

BAILIFFS have remarkably woolly powers when it comes to entering private homes and businesses. The Tribunals, Courts and Enforcement Act hands out sweeping powers to seize and sell debtors' property but offers little in the way of safeguards.

Rules can be made up as you go along. Paragraph 7 (2) of Schedule 12 to the Act leaves it up to a government minister to make regulations concerning how much notice needs to be given, what it must state and how it must be sent.

It is also left to a minister to decide whether there should be any restrictions on re-entering premises multiple times.

Paragraphs 17 and 20 provide that the bailiff may use 'reasonable force' to break into premises, and Paragraph 24 (2) allows a minister to make regulations allowing the use of violence against persons during the entry.

Under Paragraph 27, the bailiff may take with him any number of other people (who do not have to be bailiffs or police officers), and they can also use any degree of force that the bailiff is entitled to, says barrister Harry Snook.

Paragraph 25 requires that entry be effected 'at a prescribed time of day' but does not require that this time be reasonable. If anyone obstructs the bailiff, they face a fine of £2,500 and up to a year in prison under Paragraph 68 (3).

The government has ridden roughshod over our ancient rights that prevent bailiffs from breaking into homes or using force to recover civil debt. The 18th-century Prime Minister, William Pitt the Elder, said: 'The poorest man may in his cottage bid defiance to all the forces of the Crown.'

These days, Her Majesty's Courts Service says privately employed bailiffs have the right under legislation passed in 2004 to break down doors as a last resort to collect court fines.

'If a person locks himself in their home, it might be reasonable to break open the door, but probably not to smash a hole in the wall,' it advises.

Reasonable grounds for breaking down the door include the 'movement of a curtain', the sounds of a radio or a figure spotted inside which 'may be the offender'.

New powers have been proposed by ministers giving bailiffs legal backing to physically remove debtors who try to defend their property. This would include anyone who drapes themselves over a car or blocks the entrance of their home.

Diners at the Courtyard Restaurant in Havant, Hampshire, were alarmed when bailiffs stormed in and demanded they stop eating. The chef was ordered out of the kitchen and waiting customers were turned away.

The bailiffs then threatened to seize property and equipment unless owner Lynda Davis paid the 90p she owed the local council, plus £183.10 to cover costs.

'It's an extraordinarily heavy-handed action for 90p,' she said. 'I'm angry about it because this sort of thing can really hurt the reputation of a restaurant.'

Ironically, the 90p debt came about because the company processing payment for council taxes, Equita, failed to claim the extra pence on Miss Davis's cheque.

Hilary Hopgood, the revenues client manager at the council, said: 'There was a breakdown of communication. Nevertheless, what happened is regrettable.'

There were more red faces later that same day at Havant Borough Council when 'operatives' for Equita stormed into a clothes shop and ripped the store's CCTV cameras off the wall, snatched tills from the sales counter and ordered shoppers out.

Equita was obliged to issue another apology when they later discovered that the bailiffs had entered the wrong shop.

'They started stacking up equipment on the floor, anything they could take that they thought would be worth selling on, stuff they thought was valuable,' said Penny Bevington, senior property administrator for the store.

'The staff were very taken aback to say the least,' she added.

A frail 78-year-old pensioner, who had planned to contest a speeding fine but collapsed into a coma before he could lodge an appeal, was frogmarched to a cash-point machine by a bailiff just days after leaving hospital.

Retired pub landlord Andy Miller was confronted by a bailiff who threatened to remove his property by force and change the locks to his house unless he immediately paid the £60 fine, plus

£290 in costs.

'My father then agreed to be driven to get some cash. I believe he was put under duress,' said his son, Mick.

His family had earlier told Lancashire magistrates that Mr Miller had spent 10 days in a coma after suffering a combined stroke and heart attack at the Blackburn Rovers football ground.

'We made countless phone calls and sent numerous letters to the court to tell them about dad's stay in hospital,' said his son.

Unfortunately the pensioner collapsed and died outside the bank before the money could be recovered.

WATCH OUT, THERE'S A SPY ABOUT

'Surveillance is an indispensable way of gathering intelligence against terrorists and other sophisticated and ruthless criminals' – Home Office website.

Plods in pubs

A NATIONAL team of 'pub spies' has been formed to catch staff serving drinks to customers considered 'drunk'. But police have yet to give a clear definition of what constitutes being drunk despite being able to issue £80 on-the-spot fines to staff and call for a licence review.

'This could be the death of the British pub,' said Bar Entertainment & Dance Association executive director Paul Smith. 'I think it will further accelerate the shift to drinking at home.'

'It is so hard to spot a drunk and even harder to challenge them,' insists Blackpool licensee and National Association of Licensed House Managers president Dave Daly.

'In 30 years of challenging drunks, I have never known one accept the decision lightly. And if there is an altercation, will the police break their cover to help out?' he asks.

Councils around Britain are watching a pilot scheme in Somerset to fingerprint pub-goers and clubbers. Anyone wanting a pint will first have to give their name and address, date of birth, a photograph and biometric prints. Only those with a good drinking record will be allowed in.

Under the scheme, each time a person enters a pub or club, they must have their print scanned so staff can check them against a database of known 'trouble-makers'.

'The Home Office have looked at our system and are looking at trials in other towns including Coventry, Hull and Sheffield,' says Julia Bradburn, principal licensing manager at South Somerset District Council.

The council previously pioneered the fingerprinting of all drinkers in the town centre in a bid to cut disorder.

Spy in the sky I

SATELLITES are being used to check on home improvements. Images of new conservatories and garages taken from space are being used to push up council taxes and other property levies.

The images are entered on a database containing the details of every house in Britain to help tax inspectors assess new charges. Even minor improvements, invisible from the road, will be captured by aerial photographs and satellite images taken over time to spot changes.

'The public have already expressed concern at the prospect of inspectors with cameras entering their homes,' says Caroline Spelman, shadow Secretary of State for Local Government.

'For many people who need more space but can't afford to move to a bigger house, the answer is to make improvements to their existing home, but it now seems they are going to be penalised for this through council tax hikes. It's catch-22, with home-owners being taxed if they move and taxed if they don't.'

The government is compiling a database of every home in

Britain, including details of how many bedrooms each house has and what kind of roof.

Inspectors will look at whether garden sheds have been converted into offices or studios and whether kitchens or porches have been extended. The computer system will be used to assess council tax, inheritance tax and capital gains tax.

Spy in the sky II

SPY PLANES used to track the Taliban in Afghanistan could soon be turned on British citizens. Controversial government plans will see the unmanned aerial vehicles (UAVs) aid police operations around the country.

The sophisticated aircraft can gather clear images of the ground from as high as 50,000 feet. But civil liberty groups say there is a big risk that the technology will be used to spy on ordinary citizens.

Gareth Crossman of Liberty told *The Independent*: 'The question is not so much about the technology but what one does with it. We have quite definite laws about where CCTV can be used but, of course, with UAVs you have much greater ability to gather material in private spaces and this would lead to concern.'

He added: 'If they are used to simply hover to gain random information then that would obviously be a matter of worry and a civil liberty issue.'

The spy programme known as Astraea is a joint project between various government departments and defence firm BAE Systems.

Nick Miller, vice chairman of Astraea, said they are currently examining the 'technologies and procedures' that could allow unmanned air systems to operate safely and routinely in UK airspace.

'Astraea's focus is on civil applications for UAVs,' he said. 'The safe and routine operation of autonomous airborne systems promises to offer considerable public benefits, particularly in the areas of safety and security.'

Getting personal

SOME councils are now demanding intimate personal details from residents before they will empty their bins. In addition to the name of everyone in the house, they also want to know of any medical conditions.

Many families in Plymouth have been forced to nominate a member of the household who then faces a £100 fine and a criminal record if they put the wrong rubbish in the bins, put them out too soon, or put them in the wrong place.

One questionnaire asked families to provide the number of adults and children in the home and to give reasons why they might have trouble correctly placing the bins.

Other questions ask for 'reasons why a member of your household generates more rubbish than average (e.g. a medical condition)'.

The form continues: 'Please nominate an adult from your household who will take legal responsibility for your bins.'

Matthew Elliott of the Taxpayers' Alliance says: 'Councils have taken away rubbish for more than 100 years without needing to know people's medical histories, so they shouldn't be asking these intrusive questions now.'

Snoops wanted

FED UP peering from behind those old net curtains? Want to move with the times? Then why not become an unpaid snoop for Dorset police?

The force is advertising for members of the public to watch live images from street security cameras and help spot crimes and anti-social behaviour.

Applicants must be able to 'concentrate for long periods of time' and have good visual skills. Training is provided before helping man a control room in unpaid four-hour shifts.

The scheme is under way in Blandford, Shaftesbury and Gillingham, following success in Wimborne.

Inspector Phil Cheverton, section commander for North Dorset, said: 'We are looking for anyone over 18 who would like to monitor our live CCTV cameras.'

'The offer is open to as many people as possible as we don't want them to feel as though they have to come in all the time.'

The citizens' guardians will be on the look out for graffiti, public order offences, shop lifting, criminal damage, dog fouling, littering, and 'enviro-crimes'. But the recruitment plan has not proved popular with civil liberties groups.

'Increasing numbers of the general public are concerned about invasion of privacy involved with CCTV,' says Mark Wallace of the Tax-Payers Alliance.

'There will now be even fewer guarantees about the integrity and professionalism because of who is doing it.'

Speed kills

POLICE across England and Wales have been given the go-ahead to recruit civilian volunteers to man amateur speed traps. Drivers caught by the 'community speed watch' will have their details checked against the police national computer and receive warning letters.

The volunteers – who are jointly funded from police and council budgets – will be trained to use radar guns and receive advice on how best to set up 'ambush' sites. They will also be taught to use the police national computer to check vehicle details.

'This is really not a very wise thing,' says Nigel Humphries of the Association of British Drivers. 'We have seen a situation in which those operating the cameras have found themselves pointing the guns at their friends and neighbours and vice versa. They soon discover that the speeder is not some mysterious person passing through the village.'

Trails in the Cambridgeshire village of Fowlmere were called off after motorists complained that it was dividing residents and killing any community spirit.

'The final straw was when I walked by one morning and saw that they had schoolchildren on the cameras. I am the last to condone speeding but there is a question of civil liberties,' villager Salli Roskilly told *The Daily Mail*.

'None of us wants a society where we are spying on each other. There has never been a fatal accident here and I just could not see the justification for it.'

Secret Army I

COUNCILS across Britain are employing more than 1,000 'informers' to spy on members of the public. Their task is to seek out fly-tippers, tax cheats and other offenders.

Sir Christopher Rose, the Chief Surveillance Commissioner, says 429 covert human intelligence sources were 'recruited' by local authorities and government departments in 2007, with 437 the previous year.

The informants, who can be paid, pass on information about associates or even relatives flouting the rules. Each informant has a handler to watch over their safety.

'Most people would be surprised that at least one arm of the surveillance society has come under the control of local councils,' says former shadow Home Secretary David Davis. 'Everybody will expect – and it is absolutely vital – that this is controlled as tightly as any police informant would be.'

Government papers show that the covert human intelligence sources include agents, informants and officers working undercover. They can be used in a very widely defined set of circumstances, including detecting crime, protecting public health and for 'any tax, duty or levy'.

Matthew Elliott of the Taxpayers' Alliance said: 'If councils go any further down the route of paying informants, spying through net curtains and monitoring phone records, not only will our civil liberties be massively undermined but our council tax bills will go up even further.'

Secret Army II

A SECRET army of private security guards, local authority officials and civilian volunteers were quietly given police powers in 2002 to enforce on-the-spot fines for littering, dog fouling and motoring offences.

Although they have no formal police training, around 1,600 non-police officers – including traffic wardens, park keepers and housing officers – have been made part of the 'extended police family' by the Home Office under little-known legislation, the Community Safety Accreditation Schemes (CSAS).

Anyone considered to have a role in maintaining public order, including nightclub bouncers, shop staff and football stewards, can apply for the powers.

Chief constables can appoint the civilians to serve penalty notices for disorder, truancy, cycling on pavements, flouting the smoking ban, littering and dog fouling. They can also be used for seizing alcohol from under-age drinkers and can demand people's names and addresses.

A total of 1,406 staff from 95 'approved organizations', including local councils and private companies, have been given enforcement powers across all police forces in England and Wales. A further 255 people have been given powers as Vehicle Operator Services Agency Inspectors who can stop vehicles for 'the purpose of testing'. They also have the right to stop cars and inspect tax discs.

According to the Home Office: 'CSAS supports Neighbourhood Policing by building links, improving communications and helping in the delivery of effective policing to neighbourhoods. Accredited Persons have a key role to play in the delivery of Neighbourhood Policing and are an important part of the extended police family.'

Dozens of private firms – including security companies – have been handed powers to issue fines for low-scale offences and can demand personal details.

On such company, Parkguard – which patrols parks, open spaces and housing estates – even has its own 'police dogs' to help deal with anti-social behaviour and the confiscation of alcohol and tobacco. The firm says the dogs are used to 'engage with youths'.

The CSAS 'enforcers' can be identified by a very small badge worn on the lapel.

They have been criticised by the Police Federation as yet another attempt to under-cut the traditional police force. Opposition parties have also criticised the powers, despite failing to notice their introduction in 2002.

'The public will be angered that the Home Office is seeking to take serious powers that should be appropriately applied by the police and encouraging them to be given not just to local councils, but also to private firms,' says Dominic Grieve, the Conservative shadow home secretary.

'The public want to see real police on the streets discharging these responsibilities, not private firms who may use them inappropriately – including unnecessarily snooping on the lives of ordinary citizens.'

Kids under cover

CHIILDREN have been used to great effect by Hitler, Stalin and Pol Pot to inform on and denounce adults. Now councils across Britain are recruiting junior sleuths to gather evidence of minor infractions and some are receiving cash rewards of up to £500.

In a survey conducted by the *Daily Telegraph*, one in six councils said they had signed up teams of 'environment volunteers' to photograph or video neighbours guilty of dog fouling, littering or 'bin crimes'.

Known in the murky council underworld as 'covert human intelligence sources', children are also being asked to pass on the names of 'guilty' neighbours or take down their number-plates.

London's Ealing Council employs 'hundreds' of 'Junior Street Watchers', aged 8-10 years, who work under code names. Harlow Council has 25 'Street Scene Champions' aged between 11 and 14.

'They are encouraged to report the aftermath of 'envirocrimes' such as vandalism to bus shelters, graffiti, abandoned vehicles, fly-tipping, etc. They do this via telephone or email direct to the council,' explained a spokesperson for Harlow.

In some cases, the children are fitted with sophisticated listening devices or cameras to catch shop-keepers selling cigarettes and drink to those under age.

Adult volunteers are also recruited through the small ads in local papers. There are thought to be at least 4,841 people already patrolling the streets in their spare time.

The recruitment policy has been described as 'downright sinister' by Matthew Sinclair of the TaxPayers' Alliance. 'We are deeply troubled by these developments – they are straight out of the Stasi copybook. There is a combination of ever-stricter rules and ever more draconian attempts to control people.'

The *Telegraph* contacted over 240 councils across England and Wales to discover how many 'child sleuths' were working under cover. They found that just under one in six employed children, including Luton with 600 volunteers; Southwark, south London (400); Birmingham (370); Blaenau Gwent (300); and Congleton in Cheshire (300).

Some councils ask 'operatives' to look for problems, while others are sent out on regular patrols. Many town halls said they did not encourage volunteers to confront offenders for their own safety. However, Bromley Council pays up to £500 for information if it leads to a conviction.

The paper tracked down one adult volunteer prepared to talk openly about her surveillance work. A self-declared 'busy-body', Liz Henthorn, a retired nurse of 66, is one of 120 'Street Hawk' volunteers in Enfield, north London.

'If there is a problem with fly-tipping, general bad behaviour, graffiti, etcetera, then I ring the Street Hawk person and when I do it is cleared,' she explained. 'Enfield has become a lot cleaner because of us curtain twitchers having a look around.'

Plumbers to examine children

COUNCIL workers – including plumbers and carpenters – are to be given four hour's training to spot child abuse in a controversial plan allowing unqualified staff to denounce parents if their children flinch or have difficulty sitting down.

Lincoln Council is pioneering the scheme with 200 'front-line' staff attending the half-day course. They will be issued with a checklist of signs to look out for including 'unexplained bruising' and 'scalds'.

The 'initiative' has the approval of the NSPCC. Head of policy and public affairs is Natalie Cronin. 'This training should help council workers who have a lot of contact with families to know more about how to respond if they are worried about a child's welfare,' she explains.

The plan covers all council employees who visit people's homes and those involved in sports activities. They will pay special attention to any 'reluctance to get changed' or 'discomfort when walking or sitting down'.

But some critics say identifying child abuse is not always easy and add there is a danger of already over-work social services being swamped with baseless reports.

Jean Robinson of the child welfare charity AIMS described the plan for amateur social workers as 'ludicrous'.

'The idea of council plumbers and carpenters being semi-trained and seen as some sort of child-abuse spies by the people they are supposed to be serving is rather sinister,' she says.

Doctors to point the finger

THE government is moving to break down the traditional trust between doctors and patients – together with teachers and social workers – by turning them into informers. It wants them to identify potential violent offenders for monitoring by the police and other agencies.

Ministers believe that by spotting binge-drinkers, drug addicts and young gang members early they can be placed on a national database and steered away from offending behaviour in the future.

The plans have been dubbed the *Minority Report* powers, a reference to the 2002 Tom Cruise film in which a futuristic 'pre-crime' police unit imprisons criminals before they carry out their crimes.

However, doctors, teachers and social workers fear they may be placed at risk of reprisals if they are seen as police informers.

The scheme, outlined in the government's 'Tackling Violence Action Plan', will mean redrafting the NHS's strict privacy protection rules to encourage health staff to share patients' confidential data as part of 'public interest disclosures'.

Terror 'toolkit'

THE government wants teachers to inform on pupils who show signs of Islamic radicalism and has issued instructions on how to flush out budding terrorists.

The guidelines contained in 'A Toolkit for Teachers and Schools' suggests holding classroom debates to prevent extreme views from going unnoticed. Teachers will have to decide if the views expressed are 'violent' – a move which seriously concerns some teachers' unions.

Additional instructions on un-masking right-wing extremists were added to the 'toolkit' at a late stage after concern that over-emphasis on al Qaeda could be seen as Islam-bashing.

'We're not spy-catchers,' insists Mary Bousted, general

secretary of the Association of Teachers and Lecturers. 'Teachers are not trained to deal with radicalisation.'

However, teachers' union NASUWT supports the government's moves to wipe out radicalised pupils. 'We are living in challenging and difficult times which require concerted action if we are to overcome the threat of violent extremism, prejudice and bigotry,' says general secretary Chris Keates.

'Extremist groups are seeking to target young people in order to recruit and exploit them for their pernicious purposes.'

Secret squirrels

THE existence of a secret police unit formed to spy on political groups and environment campaigners came to light when they advertised for someone to head the new 'Confidential Intelligence Unit' based at Scotland Yard.

With a brief to concentrate on 'domestic extremists' and build a detailed picture of radical campaigners, the CIU's role is similar to the Cold War 'counter subversion' functions of MI5.

The job ad calls for someone to work closely with government departments, university authorities and private sector companies to 'remove the threat of criminality and public disorder that arises from domestic extremism'.

The unit's main task will be to infiltrate 'extremist groups' from climate change campaigners to the United Kingdom Independence Party. Its operatives will be protected from prosecution by Public Interest Immunity Certificates and its operations will be kept top secret.

SOMEONE TO WATCH OVER US

The Regulation of Investigatory Powers Act (RIPA) legislates for using methods of surveillance and information gathering to help the prevention of crime, including terrorism' – Home Office website.

TIM JOYCE and Jenny Paton had a funny feeling they were being watched. For two weeks Poole Borough Council kept tabs on their every movement. They even had the kids under observation.

The council invoked Britain's tough new anti-terror laws to secretly monitor the family because it was feared they had been cheating the school catchment system.

'We all know there has to be scrutiny of applications but they could carry it out without resorting to anti-terror legislation and spying,' said Miss Paton. 'This kind of scrutiny is hugely disproportionate. They could have asked for utility bills instead.'

The couple have two houses and waited until after the council deadline for school applications before moving from one address to the other. But after two weeks of surveillance, the couple were exonerated and their daughter was awarded a place.

Local authorities now have the same powers as the security services to spy on tax-payers' telephone records, emails and other highly personal data in their bid to prosecute what many describe as 'petty' crimes, from under-age smoking to littering.

Around 1,400 requests are made each day to access people's private telephone and e-mail records by public bodies, equal to 500,000 requests in 2008 or one for every 78 adults - a rise of 44 percent over two years.

RIPA was introduced in 2000 and makes provision for the 'interception of communications; the acquisition and disclosure of data relating to communications; the carrying out of surveillance; the use of covert human intelligence sources; and access to electronic data protected by encryption or passwords'.

MPs passed the Act to help police and security services combat serious crime and terrorism but in recent years nearly 800 public bodies have been quietly added to the list of those allowed to use it for covert surveillance and personal communications interception.

Many critics say the law has spiralled out of control with junior town hall officials now able to authorise spying missions without the oversight of a judge.

'Measures that were intended to fight terrorism and organised crime have instead been used to snoop on ordinary people's children, dogs and bins,' says Chris Huhne of the Liberal Democrats.

'Surveillance powers are too easily abused by over-zealous officials on the hundreds of public authorities entitled to use them,' he stressed.

Figures released by councils under the Freedom of Information Act show that thousands of people have had their telephone and e-mail records accessed.

It is estimated that about 3,000 people were targeted in the 12 months up to June 2008 for alleged offences that included dog smuggling, storing petrol without permission and keeping unburied animal carcasses.

Poole council admitted using RIPA laws on six occasions in total and said it had spied on three families suspected of fraudulent school place applications. It said two offers of school places were withdrawn as a result.

The council's actions were described as 'over the top' by Mick Brookes of the National Association of Head Teachers.

'I would have thought that if there was a doubt about where parents were living then the school would actually get in touch with them to check their address,' he suggested.

RIPA does have its supporters. Sir Paul Kennedy, the curiously-titled Interception of Communications Commissioner, believes councils should 'make much more use' of their powers.

'Very few local authorities have used their powers to acquire itemised call records in relation to the investigations which they have conducted,' he claims. 'Indeed, our inspections have shown that generally the local authorities could make much more use of communications data as a powerful tool to investigate crime.'

The increased powers have been warmly welcomed by local

authorities in their crusade against people suspected of crimes such as benefit fraud, fly-tipping and dog fouling.

Sir Simon Milton, chairman of the Local Government Association, insists that without these powers 'councils would not be able to provide the level of reassurance and protection local people demand and deserve'.

The information spy-way

GREATER powers are in the pipeline for local councils and health authorities to gain easier access to e-mail and internet records via a central government database. The Home Office says the move will mean internet service providers storing one billion incidents of data each day.

The new rules emanate from a European directive requiring all personal data to be collected across all EU states following the terrorist attacks in London in July 2005.

British taxpayers now have to pay £46 million a year to internet service providers for holding information, even though some already keep similar records for marketing purposes.

Records of every e-mail, internet session, online purchase and telephone call made over the internet will be stored for a minimum of 12 months with police, local councils and other organisations able to access the details.

The information will include the date and times of the log-in and log-off from the internet – the 'who, when, and where' of communication – but not the contents of calls, and messages or lists of websites accessed.

The Home Office says: 'The directive rightly refers to atrocities in London in making the case for adopting the measures for the retention of communication data across Europe.'

Those with access include the emergency services, the Serious Organised Crime Agency, every local council and health authority, the Post Office, Home Office, Ministry of Defence, Health and Safety Executive, and Food Standards Agency.

A spokesperson said that historic communications data was a vital tool to investigations and intelligence gathering in support of national security and crime.

'This data allows investigators to identify suspects, examine their contacts, establish relationships between conspirators and place them in a specific location at a certain time,' he said.

Add 'Home Secretary' as friend?

THE Home Office believes organised criminals and terrorists are communicating secretly on personal networking sites like Facebook and Bebo and it wants government agencies to have full access to people's personal files.

'Criminal terrorists are exploiting free social networking sites,' says an unnamed Whitehall security official quoted in *The Guardian*. 'Criminals could use a chat facility,' he went on to point out. 'They are not actually playing the game but we can't actually get hold of the data.'

Announcing plans to give the police and security agencies access to personal data stored by a variety of web services, then Home Secretary Jacqui Smith said communications were becoming 'increasingly complex and fragmented' but said additional legislation would 'make it possible, one way or another, to collect it and store it'.

'People have many accounts and sign up as Mickey Mouse and no one knows who they are,' explained another Whitehall source. 'We have to do something.'

The secret government electronic eavesdropping centre GCHQ is expected to play a large part in the plans because of their huge information storage capacity. However, private sub-contractors are also being considered as part of a package to gather data, including that held by gaming websites such as Ladbrokes and Littlewoods Bingo.

What's in your computer?

POLICE no longer need a warrant to hack into people's personal computers. Anyone suspected of committing a 'serious' crime can have their emails, web browsing habits and stored data inspected via 'remote searching'.

An amendment to the Computer Misuse Act 1990 legalises hacking if carried out by the State. Over 190 clandestine hacks were carried out in 2008, according to the Association of Chief Police Officers (Acpo).

'To be a valid authorisation, the officer giving it must believe that when it is given it is necessary to prevent or detect serious crime,' says Acpo. A serious crime is defined as an offence carrying a custodial sentence of three years and above.

'These are very intrusive powers – as intrusive as someone busting down your door and coming into your home,' points out Shami Chakrabarti, director of Liberty.

There are three main ways that the police can access personal computers. They can enter a person's home and plant a 'key-logging' device that records every key-stroke and transmits the data directly to police computers. They can also send an email containing 'malware' that allows 'remote' access, or they can park outside and tap into the suspect's wi-fi network.

Under EU legislation, any European police force can request a hacking operation on British subjects.

WATCH AROUND THE CLOCK

'Every move you make, Every bond you break, Every step you take, I'll be watching you' – The Police.

BRITONS are monitored 24 hours a day, every day. Each time they click a mouse or pick up a mobile their movements are logged.

Every time they swipe a card or travel by road, rail, sea or air, State agencies and their corporate counterparts are watching every step of the way.

In 2008, the average person had around 160,000 separate pieces of personal information noted, logged and stored on databases, both public and private.

Grandmother Lynn Pierce was tracked down to her home by the Tesco loyalty card she earlier used to buy flowers for her mother's grave. When a keen-eyed security guard spotted Lynn on CCTV tucking a scarf into her handbag, he was quick to call police.

Two days later they showed up at her door. 'It was absolutely terrible,' she said. 'I've never done anything wrong in my life and there they were accusing me of shoplifting.'

She told the *Daily Mail* of her disgust that Tesco had used the information on her loyalty card and handed it to police. 'All I did was put my scarf in my handbag while I was looking for my glasses,' she explained.

'I'd rather they had spoken to me there and then. It would have been a nasty shock but at least they would have realised I hadn't taken anything.'

Tesco offered coupons worth £50 in compensation.

The price of loyalty

BRITONS hold around 25 million Tesco loyalty cards, representing 14 million households, according to *The New Statesman*.

'Shortly before its fall, the German Democratic Republic police state had a population of around 16 million. In all probability, Tesco holds more files on British citizens than the East German State held on its people.'

The store's database holds the name, age, address, telephone number and email of every card holder. It knows what they like to eat and what they don't.

It can deduce lifestyles from shopping preferences, and tell whether customers buy excessive numbers of condoms and if they have a penchant for cooking sherry. It also knows if they have ever complained to Tesco about anything.

'The information helps Tesco to typecast its customers by analysing their "life stage", whether student, young family or retired,' says the paper. 'It assesses how much they are worth to them, by spending and loyalty. It works out if they are "upmarket", "market" or "poor".'

'Being able to classify groups in this way has helped Tesco become the UK's dominant retailer,' it says.

The *New Statesman* expressed serious concern when the government announced that it was proposing to link the data contained on supermarket loyalty cards to the compulsory biometric identity cards.

With social services now calling for obese children to be taken away from their parents and put into care, such a link should be a major cause for concern.

David Rogers, spokesperson on public health for the Local Government Association, says councils may have to act if they believe parents are putting children's health in danger with poor diets. Access to their weekly shopping list could easily provide the evidence needed.

'Councils would step in to deal with an under-nourished and neglected child so should a case with a morbidly obese child be different?' he asked.

Such a merger would also allow data traffic to move in both directions, between the government and major corporations including banks and supermarkets.

'Information contained on the national identity database, set up to underpin the ID card scheme, would be made available to companies for a price,' explained the paper.

The spy in your pocket

THE mobile telephone is the perfect tracking device. It can also listen in on conversations even when switched off. Every call and every text is logged by the network provider, including who was called and when, as well as the caller's location. The contacts book is easily accessible.

The users' movements can be followed in real time as the device is tracked by triangulation from phone masts. Phones can also be tracked when switched off as each device emits a unique identifying signal at regular intervals. All this information can be accessed by police and other public authorities investigating 'crimes'.

Surveillance staff at a Portsmouth shopping centre are using the technology to track customers' movements. By gathering mobile phone signals, staff can see which shops and facilities customers visit and for how long.

The centre does not have to inform customers about the technology because it does not capture any personal information.

Gunwharf operations manager Peter Emery said: 'We are experimenting with a new technology. We can find out which of our toilets are most popular and if a shop is attracting a lot of customers.'

Type the words 'mobile tracking' into a search engine and over 2.5 million services are available to track people's mobile movements, from keeping tabs on the kids and following a cheating partner, to tracking a potential witness.

Private investigators say spouses who suspect their partner of cheating are increasingly using mobile phone tracking websites.

Sharp edge to Bluetooth

BLUETOOTH signals are being used to covertly track tens of thousands of Britons without their consent in an experiment which has installed scanners at secret locations in offices, campuses, streets and pubs to pinpoint people's whereabouts.

According to *The Guardian*, the scanners – the first 10 of which were installed in Bath in 2005 – are capturing Bluetooth radio signals from mobile phones, laptops and digital cameras.

The data is being used in a project called Cityware to study how people move around cities. But people are not being told that their devices could be providing a permanent record of their journeys which is then stored on a central database.

According to Eamonn O'Neill, Cityware's director: 'The objective is not to track individuals, whether by Bluetooth or any other means. We are interested in the aggregate behaviour of city dwellers as a whole.'

But he insists: 'The notion that any agency would seriously consider Bluetooth scanning as a surveillance technique is ludicrous.'

This is not a view shared by some privacy experts who point out that each device has a unique code that identifies the user. The Information Commissioner has warned the public to 'think carefully' before switching on their Bluetooth signals.

'To assert that there aren't privacy implications demonstrates an astonishing disregard for consumer rights,' says Simon Davies, director of Privacy International.

He says the technology could well become the CCTV of the mobile industry. 'If the technology is as safe as they claim, then all the technical specifications should be published and people should be informed when they are being tracked,' he added.

The technology is reminiscent yet again of the futuristic film *Minority Report*. Bluetooth tracking is already being used to aim advertisements at people as they walk past shops or billboards.

Critics slam Oysters

GOVERNMENT agencies can access travel data transmitted by 'smart card' tickets to follow an individual's movements across the capital or further afield. When Transport for London introduced the 'Oyster card' system in 2003 civil rights campaigners expressed grave concerns.

Each card has a unique ID number for each registered owner and provides a complete breakdown of their journeys whenever the card is used. Anyone buying a season ticket – and those paying by credit card – have their details logged.

Oyster cards are read when placed next to a reading device. When the card is presented at a tube station or on a bus, the ID number, together with information including the location and time of the transaction, is sent from the card reader to a central database.

Under the raft of terror laws, State agencies can access this stored data and use it to track people's movements. John Monk of the Oyster project admits that it is 'likely the information would be used for court evidence'.

However, the security behind the card is seriously flawed, as demonstrated by Dutch scientists who say anyone can clone an Oyster card with a basic laptop computer.

Bart Jacobs of Radboud University used a cloned card to enter public buildings in the Netherlands. He then travelled to London and spent a day on the Underground without paying.

The Oyster employs a Mifare smartcard which is also used for access to thousands of schools, hospitals and government departments around Britain. About ten million Mifare smartcards are sold in the UK each year.

Travel prints

PASSENGERS using Britain's airports are to be fingerprinted for both international and domestic flights. An earlier attempt to introduce the measure was condemned by the Information Commissioner as potentially illegal under data protection laws.

The amendments to national aviation security rules will require fingerprints to be scanned when passengers pass through security into the airside terminal. Passengers will be fingerprint-scanned again at their flight departure gate.

The government hopes to expand the scheme to cover major seaports and the Channel Tunnel rail links.

Police and the security services will be able to check fingerprints against international watch lists and Interpol databases, searching for suspects travelling on false identities.

The Information Commissioner's Office was highly critical of an earlier attempt to introduce the system at Heathrow and recommended that passengers asked to give their fingerprints should only do so 'under protest'.

The changes are being introduced under existing legislation, without the need for a debate in Parliament. The same method has been used to introduce the compulsory production of ID for people travelling between mainland Britain and Northern Ireland.

The move formulises an 'internal border' within the UK and critics warn that it could pave the way for identity checks on all domestic flights and ferries in Britain.

The Home Office is considering police and security service requests for wider access to information on passenger movements within Britain, including air, sea, rail and coach networks.

Permission to leave, please

ANYONE wishing to leave the country will have to give the government 24-hours notice or face fines up to £5,000 under the e-Borders scheme that comes fully into effect in 2010.

The UK Border Agency wants passengers to supply credit card details, email addresses, holiday contact numbers and detailed travel itinerary as well as listing all previously missed flights.

People leaving Britain will be forced to hand over 53 separate pieces of information when they pay for their ticket. Details will be shared between police, HM Revenue and Customs and domestic and foreign security services.

Those failing to complete all the questions or anyone deemed 'suspicious' will be prevented from leaving.

All airlines, ferry companies, rail operators and travel agencies will be obliged to provide comprehensive information on every passenger which will then be stored on a new database and be used to 'profile' suspects.

Even swimmers attempting to cross the Channel and their support teams will be subject to the rules along with weekend sailors, sea fishermen and day-trippers. The owners of light aircraft will also be brought under the system, which will eventually track 250 million journeys annually, with an initial budget of £1.2 billion.

It is unclear if people who deviate from their travel plans will face prosecution.

'The UK has one of the toughest borders in the world and we are determined to ensure it stays that way,' says immigration minister Phil Woolas. 'Our high-tech electronic borders system will allow us to count all passengers in and out and targets those who aren't willing to play by our rules.'

In an early sign of function creep, ministers also want to prevent people leaving the country if they have any outstanding fines. The details have been outlined in an 'explanatory memorandum' to the Immigration and Asylum Act prepared by the Home Office.

Officials say the e-Borders scheme could help recoup millions of pounds of unpaid fines – including those for 'bin crimes' and motoring offences – and make it easier to confiscate criminals' assets by barring them from leaving the country.

CCTV: EVERYBODY SMILE

'George Orwell was not quite right: the technology revolution he foresaw is not a controlling force enslaving people, but for the most part a liberating force empowering them' – Gordon Brown.

IN 1785 Jeremy Bentham invented the perfect prison which he called the Panopticon.

The principle was simple: a single jailer sat in a central hub – rather like a spider at the centre of its web – and watched all the prisoners. They could not see him.

The beauty of the system was that the inmates could never tell if they were being watched, so they acted as if they were.

'As the watchmen cannot be seen, they need not be on duty at all times, effectively leaving the watching to the watched,' explained Bentham at the time.

George Orwell adapted the idea for his dystopian novel *1984*, where citizens were never sure if the telescreen in the corner was watching them or not.

Today, we have closed circuit television – perhaps as many as one for every 12 people in the country – around 4.5 million cameras in total. But no one knows for sure.

An individual in an urban area can be captured by more than 300 separate cameras on any given day. They stare into some people's homes and they follow us all as we go about our daily business.

Few public places are without cameras. Numerous State agencies from MI5 to local authorities operate CCTV cameras, as do private companies.

The police have branched out and now send specialist video units to anti-government and anti-corporate protests and they keep extensive databases of those involved.

'Even if no crime or public order offence has been committed, the footage is kept by the police, providing evidence of an individual's political stance on issues such as the war in Iraq, nuclear energy, pensioners' rights and hunting,' says Richard Tyler of UKwatch.net.

A new generation of smart cameras now have their eyes on the populace. Some have listening devices while others can issue commands. A growing number now use face recognition software.

There are also a host of Automatic Number Plate Recognition (ANPR) cameras around the country that automatically read every passing number plate and pass it on to the Police National Computer.

The national network of roadside cameras can capture 50 million licence plates a day, giving police the power to reconstruct almost every motorist's journey. The details are recorded and stored at a multi-million pound data centre in Hendon, North London, for investigations ranging from terrorism to low-level crime.

Police have been encouraged to 'fully and strategically exploit' the database, according to an ANPR strategy document seen following a Freedom of Information request.

Civil liberties groups say the database significantly increases intrusion into individuals' private lives. Simon Davies, director of Privacy International, says the database gives the authorities 'extraordinary powers of surveillance' that were 'unnecessary and disproportionate'.

'This would never be allowed in any other democratic country,' he said, adding: 'This is possibly one of the most valuable reserves of data imaginable.'

Local authorities have also adapted their CCTV cameras to capture licence plates on behalf of police. Infrared cameras that can read licence plates from 2,000 feet have been installed in police helicopters, while patrol cars have been equipped with mobile cameras.

The government holds great store in 24-hour surveillance as a panacea for all crime, from anti-social behaviour and dog fouling, right up to tax evasion and terrorism. Gordon Brown says CCTV is there to safeguard our liberties.

'To say that we should ignore the new demands of security, to assume that the laws and practises which have applied in the past are sufficient always to face the future... that would be the politics of complacency,' he insists.

Compared to other Western countries, Britain's citizens are the most closely watched. In a 36 nation survey, Privacy International found that the UK came fifth from last – but above Malaysia and

China – with 'endemic surveillance' and the worst record for protecting individual privacy.

'We have more CCTV cameras and we have looser laws on privacy and data protection,' insists Dr David Murakami-Wood of the Surveillance Studies Network, who says things can only get worse.

'People's lives will be monitored even more in the next decade by the government, the public sector, employers and big business.'

Ministry of Funny Walks

PEOPLES' 'behavioural oddities' can now be analysed by 'Intelligence Pedestrian Surveillance' software that identifies crimes even before they happen.

The government has spent over £500,000 developing cameras with 'gait recognition' that recognise if people are walking suspiciously or strangely. A human operator is then alerted.

The IPS system is already connected to a number of CCTV cameras, allowing people's movements to be reduced to a series of pixels and compared to a pre-defined set of patterns or algorithms.

Early versions of the system can detect loitering, abandoned packages, graffiti or vandalism, overcrowding and other suspicious behaviour. It can also be used to prevent suicides and all forms of 'anti-social' behaviour.

Murmurs of discontent

ARTIFICIAL intelligence software now allows CCTV camera to 'hear' crimes and then capture them on film. Researchers say the system can recognise sounds such as breaking glass, shouting or crowds gathering.

Super-swift cameras can then swing towards the noise in 300 milliseconds – the time it takes a person to turn their head if they hear a scream. The software may eventually be able to identify words that 'suggest a crime' and possibly even murmurs of discontent.

The government-sponsored project at Portsmouth University's institute of industrial research also aims to develop 'visual pattern programs' that raise the alarm if someone lifts their arm suddenly or starts running.

Dr David Brown, director of the institute, says: 'The longer artificial intelligence is in the software the more it learns. Later versions will get cleverer as time goes on, perhaps eventually being able to identify specific words being said.'

Spy in the wall

COUNCIL bin police are now employing special miniature cameras that can be hidden in baked bean tins and household bricks to nab householders who flout strict rules on recycling and rubbish collection.

London's Ealing council is already using the technology to catch people committing a range of 'crimes' and says anyone breaking the rules on rubbish disposal would be named and shamed as an 'enviro-criminal'.

The cameras, which cost £200 each, are activated by movement and can e-mail images to the council's CCTV control centre.

'We have three mobile, disguised cameras at our disposal,' admitted a council spokesperson. 'They are deployed where a major 'enviro-crime' issue has been identified.'

Although the council says the cameras were 'unlikely' to be used on householders, it could not rule out the possibility.

Perils of the dump

HOUSEHOLDERS taking a trip to the dump risk having their every move followed by a sophisticated CCTV system capable of reading and storing car number plates to identify who are using the rubbish tips, how often, and what they are throwing away.

The government is putting pressure on local councils to cut the amount of rubbish sent to landfill sites. People moving house – and throwing away unused items – are particularly at risk from council snoopers. Many fear the added surveillance will lead to more illegal fly-tipping.

The internet-controlled cameras are being installed at waste sites across the country. Several councils say they will use camera evidence to mount prosecutions – raising fears that more house-holders will be taken to court over what they throw away.

Cameras have been installed in Buckinghamshire, Croydon, Somerset, Dundee and Hertfordshire, and more councils are planning to follow suit after the £80 million-a-year Waste and Resources Action Programme quango suggested they use CCTV to 'check vehicles visiting dumps repeatedly'.

Cameras were imposed after the government introduced a penalty of £150 a tonne on local authorities that dump too much waste in landfill sites.

We can't see inside

ISLINGTON butcher Maurice Wood was concerned that the CCTV camera on a 70 foot pole outside his house was watching inside, including in his young daughter's bedroom.

When he woke up one morning and pulled back the curtains, he was shocked to see the camera looking back at him. 'My daughter has even had the camera pointing towards her bedroom,' he said.

And while he insists he is in favour of CCTV to deter crime, he adds: 'There is nothing more unnerving and distressing than having a camera aimed at your home.'

Neighbour Jessamy Corbett was also concerned the camera was spying on her family.

'We have a right to absolute privacy in our own homes,' she

said. 'I've no issue with CCTV. But I do have an issue about it looking into my bedroom. We want it taken away and put where there's no potential to intrude.'

But a council spokesperson said: 'We have explained to Mr Wood and Ms Corbett that we use sophisticated technology at the control room to block their windows from the camera's view. I'd like to reassure residents that this camera is there to keep them safer.'

We can, but we're not looking

ONE 25-year-old woman discovered that council staff had been using the CCTV outside her home to watch her naked after police arrived and showed a film of her undressing.

In a statement heard by the jury at Liverpool Crown Court, the unnamed woman said her privacy had been taken away.

'I was contacted by Merseyside Police and I was informed that the CCTV camera outside my flat had been used to view incidents inside,' she said. 'The next day I was shown a CD of the recordings taken by staff at Sefton Council.'

Over several hours, she was filmed cuddling her boyfriend before undressing, using the toilet, having a bath and watching television dressed only in a towel.

'I didn't give anybody any permission to watch me and I feel very upset and angry,' she said. 'I feel my privacy has been taken away and that someone has been inside my flat without my permission.'

Kevin Judge, 42, and David Welsh, 41, who both worked in the CCTV control centre for Sefton Metropolitan Borough Council, denied charges of voyeurism.

Mr Judge admitted misconduct but denied voyeurism on the grounds he did not point the camera or view the images for sexual gratification. Mr Welsh also denied misconduct and claimed he never saw any improper image because he was too busy.

A spokesperson for Sefton Council said the internal

safeguards had vindicated the council because the culprits were apprehended. And he reassured residents that 'we will not tolerate an abuse of position from any of our staff or accept such a failure to meet the high standards of behaviour and professionalism we expect'.

Over exposure

TWO YOUNG women found themselves dragged through the courts after a CCTV operator had them arrested for showing their breasts on Worthing seafront. The case was eventually laughed out of court.

Their troubles began when they took a stroll on the beach with a group of friends. After a few drinks, they decided to flash at the CCTV camera as a joke – but the operator failed to see the funny side and called police.

When officers arrived, both women were arrested, questioned and then charged with committing an act 'outraging public decency' – an offence which carries a maximum sentence of six months prison or a £5,000 fine.

'It was just a little joke, one of those spur-of-the-moment things,' said Abbi-Louise Maple, 21. 'It's a waste of time and money. They should be concentrating on drug dealers and rapists, not two girls having a bit of harmless fun.'

If the case had gone to trial at crown court it would have cost the taxpayer £8,000 a day.

Rachel Marchant, also 21, said: 'We did not intend to upset anyone and I don't think it's that offensive because people sunbathe topless all the time.'

There are no laws prohibiting nudity in public, although people can be prosecuted under the common law offence of outraging public decency if it causes harassment, alarm or distress.

Kids in the can

A PRIVATE company is installing CCTV cameras and microphones in classrooms to compile 'evidence' of bad behaviour that can be used in court. The Classwatch cameras are fitted in around 85 schools and colleges and film children as young as four.

The equipment costs around £3,000 per classroom or can be leased for £50 a month, and includes ceiling-mounted microphones and cameras and even Crown Prosecution Service-approved 'evidence bags'.

The company's £30,000-a-year chairman is Tim Loughton, Conservative MP for Worthing East and Shoreham, and Shadow Children's Minister.

His firm says the system provides 'impartial witnesses' that can curb bullying and unruly behaviour. It also acts as a safeguard for teachers accused of abuse.

But Martin Johnson, deputy general secretary of the Association of Teachers and Lecturers (ATL), says: 'We strongly object to schools or colleges having free rein to use CCTV and microphones, especially in sensitive areas such as classrooms, changing rooms and toilets. We expect CCTV to be used appropriately and not to spy on staff or pupils.'

A survey of teachers found the majority believe their schools are fitted with surveillance cameras and almost a quarter feared further cameras lay hidden around the grounds.

Nearly 10 percent of teachers polled by the ATL said there were cameras in the lavatories. More than 7 percent said there were cameras in their classrooms and over 15 percent said they had more than 20 cameras in their school.

Supporters say the cameras protect children and staff. But Dr Mary Bousted of the ATL said there were no rules governing the installation of the cameras or the use of images.

'No one really knows enough about the use of CCTV in schools – it's a very new issue,' she said.

The Association's president, Julia Neal, also condemned the 'over-measured, over-monitored' education system, warning that the increasingly 'Orwellian tactics' would see lessons become uniform and uninspiring if staff were worried about being observed.

Almost half of teachers said they were used personally to monitor pupil behaviour and said they would behave differently if they knew CCTV was operating.

Robo-Wardens

MANY local councils are testing new head-mounted video cameras which are being given to traffic wardens and 'school crossing patrollers'.

Greater Manchester now employs 20 'super wardens'. Although their main task is to issue traffic penalties, they have extra powers to issue on-the-spot fines for anti-social behaviour.

Local authorities were given greater powers to tackle 'crime' under the Clean Neighbourhoods Act 2006. Salford Council's wardens issue penalties up to £80 for offences which include littering, fly-posting and dog-fouling.

NCP – the private company that controls the wardens – will use the film as evidence to back up their wardens if any fine is challenged and also in the event of an attack or abuse.

'We are more than happy to work with the police and pass on any evidence we gather. It can only help them to have people out on the streets with a camera all the time,' said James Pritchard of NCP.

Eye on oldies

THE CCTV in the Yates bar in Newcastle-Under-Lyme had difficulty seeing the face of an 81-year-old pensioner so staff ordered him to remove his flat cap to give the camera a better view. A bartender told pensioner Harvey Talbot that the cap could hide his face if he committed a crime.

'I told him I was 81 and couldn't move that fast because my legs are bad and what trouble am I going to cause at my age?' said Mr Talbot. 'I could understand it if I was a violent person causing trouble but I do not have a blemish on my record.'

Yates defended their action by saying they were only following advice from Staffordshire Police. However, the force said a dress code was not their responsibility.

Pubs applying for new licenses or attempting to renew old ones are often finding that they must first agree to install CCTV and give police full access.

'I was stunned,' says Islington publican Nick Gibson of the Draper's Arms, 'to find that the police were prepared to approve – i.e. not fight – our licence on condition that we installed CCTV, capturing the head and shoulders of everyone coming into the pub, to be made available to them on request.'

A spokesperson for the Metropolitan Police, while denying the move was outright police policy, said: 'Individual boroughs may impose blanket rules in support of their objectives to prevent crime and disorder and to assist the investigation of offences when they do occur.'

In a letter to *The Guardian*, Mr Gibson said he has 'been spitting teeth in a silent rage since I first heard of this request'.

'At every turn, I am alternately advised to keep my head down or laughed at for my naivety for thinking that the world was ever not thus,' he wrote. 'When was it that the constant small erosion of our liberties became irreversible?'

Enough

A PENSIONER concerned that CCTV cameras infringed his civil liberties has been fined after launching a leaflet campaign against intrusive surveillance.

Keith Sharp, 68, of Dawlish, was handed the fixed penalty notice for putting 4,000 leaflets through neighbours' doors complaining about the £80,000 surveillance system in his neighbourhood.

Police issued Mr Sharp with the £80 fine as they said his leaflets – which likened the local council with Hitler's Germany – caused 'harassment, alarm and distress within the community'.

Mr Sharp, a retired journalist and writer, is to leave Britain and begin a new life in Argentina.

'I have wanted to get away from these wretched spy cameras for a while. I do not like being spied upon,' he explained. 'I hope people will carry on the fight against Big Brother Britain.'

AN EYE ON THE KIDS

'If I wanted to create a surveillance society, I would start by creating dossiers on kindergarten children so that the next generation could not comprehend a world without surveillance' – Andre Bacard, author of 'The Computer Privacy Handbook'.

GARY PUGH loves children so much that he wants to keep them all in a very large database. As director of forensic sciences at Scotland Yard and DNA spokesperson for the Association of Chief Police Officers, Mr Pugh is in a good position to carry out his plan.

A nation-wide database of all children would help cut crime in the future he says because those with criminal tendencies can be weeded out early on and appropriate action taken.

'If we have a primary means of identifying people before they offend, then in the long-term the benefits of targeting younger people are extremely large,' he says. 'You could argue the younger the better.'

He admits his views may be considered controversial and bemoans the fact that universal sampling – everyone being forced to give their genetic samples to the database – is currently prohibited by cost and logistics.

The Institute for Public Policy Research also believes that prevention should start young. 'Prolific offenders typically began offending between the ages of 10 and 13,' it points out. 'Suspect' children could then be targeted with 'cognitive behavioural therapy', parenting programmes and intensive support.

High-profile cases such as the death of Baby P and the 'kidnapping' of Sharon Matthews add fuel to the government's call for new legislation to probe ever deeper into family affairs. But Chris Davis of the National Primary Headteachers' Association believes moves to log and label children from birth should be treated with suspicion.

'It could be seen as a step towards a police state,' he says. 'It is condemning them at a very young age to something they have not yet done. They may have the potential to do something, but we all have the potential to do things. To label children at that stage and put them on a register is going too far.'

In 2007, Tony Blair announced plans that would see all children undergo tests to see if they risk becoming criminals in later life. Universal checks are needed throughout a child's development, he explained, to help service providers identify those most at risk of offending.

At the time, Tony Blair admitted many people might be uneasy with the idea of intervening so intrusively into family life but said there was no point 'pussy-footing'. He said action could even be taken 'pre-birth' if necessary.

'If you've got someone who is a teenage mum, not married, not in a stable relationship ... here is the support we are prepared to offer you, but we do need to keep a careful watch on you and how your situation is developing because all the indicators are that your type of situation can lead to problems in the future,' he said.

And there could be sanctions for parents who refused to take advice, he added.

Child snatchers

PAULINE Goodwin was surprised when two visitors turned up to see her new-born baby just hours after giving birth. Instead of flowers they brought papers for her to sign and then demanded she hand over her baby daughter.

'They said that because the baby had never lived in a family unit, she didn't have a bond with us so it didn't matter if she was taken away,' said Pauline. 'I don't know where she is now and I'm not entitled to know.'

Ironically, Pauline opened the door to social services soon after her ten-year abusive marriage broke down and she asked for help.

'They started visiting two or three times a day and phoning the children's schools daily,' she said. 'Social workers turned up during the middle of one of the children's birthday parties and sometimes would arrive to carry out spot-checks at 10pm, shining torches into the sleeping children's faces.'

Liberal Democrat MP John Hemming who chairs the Justice for Families group strongly believes newborn babies are being removed from their parents in order for councils to meet government adoption targets.

'What is utterly unacceptable...is the clear evidence that social workers are literally snatching newborn babies and children from good, stable, loving homes,' he says. 'I have great difficulty in understanding how what has been done has benefited any of these people.'

He is particularly concerned that an increasing number of very small babies are being taken into care.

'This may seem an outrageous allegation, yet how else to explain newborn babies literally being torn from their mother's arms on no other grounds than that the mother 'might' get post-natal depression, or that the child is 'at risk of emotional abuse' in the future?'

The MP says he knows of over 1,000 similar cases, including that of Sam Thomas, 19, who was forced to flee her home in

Somerset and go to Ireland. She feared social services were planning to seize her newborn child and have it adopted.

Alarm bells sounded when she discovered social workers had told the hospital not to let her leave the maternity ward with her child 'under any circumstances' without their say-so. No court order was ever sought.

'All I want is the opportunity to prove I can be a fit mother – but I feel like I'm on the run,' said Sam, who has no history of endangering children. 'It's the only way to make sure I can have my baby girl and be with her in peace.'

She says Somerset County Council social services have made her out to be an unfit mother and that the data they hold on her is inaccurate. 'Everything in their reports is either wrong or out of context,' she insists. 'They're not listening to anything I've got to say.'

Tests for toddlers

CHILDREN as young as four could soon be obliged to undergo tests to determine their future mental health following guidance from the National Institute for Health and Clinical Excellence (Nice).

It says schools have a duty to improve children's emotional and psychological well-being and must combat factors that are 'likely to lead to poor mental health or mental disorders'.

Nice says that a school's success will be measured by indicators developed by Warwick and Edinburgh universities which monitor positive attributes such as confidence, resilience, attentiveness and the ability to form good relationships.

The 'well-being scale' involves putting 14 statements to children about their thoughts and feelings and asking them whether they feel like that often, rarely, some of the time, all the time, or never.

Its use in primary schools could see data collected from thousands of pupils, from the age of four to 11. The information would then be stored on a database for future reference, profiling and possible intervention.

According to the Office of National Statistics, one in 10 children under the age of 16 have a clinically diagnosed mental disorder.

Boys are generally more likely to have mental problems than girls and mental illness is more prevalent among children from disrupted families, those whose parents have no educational qualifications and those from poorer families and living in disadvantaged areas.

Getting them young

CHILDREN as young as three have their profiles stored for future reference on police criminal databases even though they are too young to be charged in a criminal court.

One four-year-old was held for a drugs offence and a seven-year-old was stopped for driving carelessly. Other serious crimes where primary school pupils were thought to be 'probably responsible' include fraud, arson, racial harassment and even sex offences.

Bedfordshire Police recorded 58 crimes committed by under-10s including an assault causing harm by a three-year-old toddler in Luton. Two children aged four and five were arrested for criminal damage and a six-year-old was reported for burglary.

In Cumbria, where 44 under-10s were arrested, two four-year-olds were quizzed in connection with drugs and theft offences.

In total, there were 1,825 crimes committed by under-10s between 2007 and 2008 according to figures obtained under the Freedom of Information Act. But the figure is believed to be just the tip of the iceberg as some police forces were unable to provide statistics.

Under Home Office rules, there is no longer a requirement to log offences committed by those under the age of criminal responsibility.

In Strathclyde, Scotland, where a total of 463 under-10s were held for crimes, a three and five-year-old were blamed for vandalism while two seven-year-olds were reported for driving carelessly and being drunk.

Finger print free-for-all

SCHOOLS across the country are gathering biometric details from their pupils at an alarming rate and in many cases breaking government guidelines by not first seeking parental permission.

Critics say there is no effective monitoring of the system as no authority or government department has taken overall control.

The *Yorkshire Post* discovered at least 18 schools in its region using fingerprint identification systems, but says the true figure is likely to be well over a hundred.

The paper says only a handful of the region's 15 local education authorities had any idea of how many systems were operating in their areas and some wrongly believed none were in use at all.

Cops cast wide net

YOUNGSTERS are being targeted for arrest so their DNA profiles are ready and waiting should they commit a serious crime in the future. By making arrests for a minor offence such as criminal damage the police can take the DNA of a group of youngsters all at the same time.

The Home Office explains: 'Those who are innocent have nothing to fear from providing a sample, and retaining this evidence is no different to recording other forms of information such as photographs and witness statements.'

The State holds the details of more than 100,000 innocent children on its DNA database with the numbers growing at an alarming rate each year.

Research by Action on Rights for Children and the pressure

group GeneWatch UK – using Home Office figures – shows police have accelerated sharply the rate at which they are gathering samples from children.

Since 2004, anyone aged ten or above who is arrested in England or Wales can have their DNA and fingerprints taken without their consent. Around 80,000 innocent children are likely to be added to the database every 12 months. Parents can appeal but very few samples are ever removed.

Dr Helen Wallace, director of GeneWatch UK, said: 'Anyone with access to the DNA database can use these children's DNA profiles to trace where they have been, or who they are related to.

'Do we really trust the Home Office not to misuse this information and to safeguard it from others who may want to infiltrate the system?' she asked.

Mother of all child databases

GOVERNMENT policies designed to safeguard children are in reality exposing them to greater dangers while creating a surveillance culture with parents pushed to the sidelines, according to a report by the Information Commissioner.

The report describes the extensive databases being established in education, youth justice, health and social work, and the linking of these systems through the new Information Sharing Index, the Integrated Children's System and a new, in-depth personal profiling tool known as the 'Common Assessment Framework'.

These all come under the umbrella of the Children's Index and the 'Contact Point' computer – a supposedly confidential system intended as an early warning system for children at risk of abuse – with an initial budget of £241 million. The Children's Act 2004 gives the Secretary of State for Education the power to create a database of everyone in England under 18.

The Commission says the systems are not secure and violate UK and European data protection and human rights law. Although introduced as a response to the death of Victoria

Climbie in 2000, the policy shifts the focus away from abused children, putting them at greater risk says the report.

'When you are looking for a needle in a haystack, is it necessary to keep building bigger haystacks?' asks Richard Thomas, the Information Commissioner. 'The new IT based strategy will divert resources and attention away from these children, potentially posing more dangers.'

Files are held by many bodies on the 11 million children in England and Wales, but the index will link this sensitive information in one database accessible to hundreds of thousands of officials.

The Education Department insists there will be 'extremely strict controls' over access to the database. Education minister Lord Adonis insists 'between 300,000 and 400,000 users will access the index'. But opponents say this is well short of the mark.

Legislation governing the database lists a vast number who could potentially be granted access – potentially up to one million people. These include school administrators and 'any employee' of a police force.

'Rather than the 330,000 they have previously suggested – which was bad enough – it appears that a million or more people will be able to get access under the terms of the Children's Act,' says Phil Booth of the NO2ID privacy campaign.

'This, in the light of the government's own auditors saying that Contact Point could never be made secure, paints a deeply disturbing picture.'

Not all children in the country will find their personal details listed on Contact Point. According to the *Daily Telegraph*, a two-tier system has been devised.

'The government has now decided to give the children of 'celebrities' special safeguards to protect their privacy,' says the paper. 'Two classes of membership have been devised: one for the offspring of people who are well known, and one for just about everyone else.'

'The addresses and telephone numbers of celebrities will be

taken off the database if their children are believed to be in danger of being kidnapped.'

Robert Whelan, the deputy director of the think-tank Civitas, says the move to protect the children of pop stars and politicians underlines the general fears of most parents.

'The government is showing it has no confidence in this database,' he says.

3

WELCOME TO BRITAIN

'We will only meet the new challenges of security, of economic change, of communities under pressure by building a new relationship between citizens and government that ensures that government is a better servant of the people' – Gordon Brown.

THE average Briton is getting a very raw deal. Even before the economy tumbled, we had the second lowest quality of life in Europe. We pay more for everything and our tax bills are heftier than other European workers. We also have below average investment in health and education and we die younger.

British citizens sought better lives overseas at the rate of one every three minutes in 2007. A poll for the BBC showed more than half the population have considered emigrating in search of a better life. Some 12 percent said they did not like what Britain had become.

According to government estimates, the established 'white' population of England dropped by nearly 250,000 between 2002 and 2006. But in 2007, a record 400,000 left the country.

UK families pay much more for petrol and electricity and almost half again for domestic gas, according to the uSwitch.com quality of life index. We have only 28 days holiday a year, compared to 40 in France, and we retire later than other Europeans.

Although it found British workers had by far the highest household net income, uSwitch ranked the UK in ninth place in the ten-country survey, with only Ireland coming lower.

People blame high taxes, increased costs and strain on public services brought about by a rapidly swelling population as the main reasons to emigrate.

When it comes to 'wellbeing', Britain comes third from the bottom in Western Europe according to the New Economics Foundation, an independent think-tank.

Researchers asked 42,000 people in 22 countries around 50 questions based on two concepts: personal wellbeing, and broader social wellbeing. They reveal that young people in Britain have the lowest levels of trust and belonging in Europe, matched only in Bulgaria and Estonia.

It says one-fifth of the UK population have trouble sleeping because of economic worries. Nearly a third say they almost never wake up feeling rested. The British have the second lowest levels of energy (trailed only by Spain). Britain is also the most bored nation.

'This is what people mean when they talk about a broken society,' says Nic Marks, one of the report's co-authors. His report describes a 'myopic obsession' with money that blinds us to the negative impacts on our wellbeing, such as longer working hours and rising levels of indebtedness.

'It has created an economic system that has squeezed out opportunities for individuals, families and communities to pursue activities that promote wellbeing,' the report says.

According to the Office for National Statistics, England's population density is among the highest in the world, ranking third after Bangladesh (1,045 per sq km) and South Korea (498 per sq km). In 2008, the number of people in every square kilometre in England was 395. Official projections say the population will be squeezed tighter in the future, with 464 people for every square kilometre by 2031. The United Nations predicts that Britain will overtake Germany as Europe's most populous nation by 2050.

But government population statistics are opaque at best. MPs on the Treasury Select Committee say the methods used to estimate immigration are 'not fit for purpose'.

'It is now impossible to estimate accurately the UK population today,' insists committee chairman Michael Fallon, who says such figures are essential for any government allocating money for public services. 'Unreliable statistics make planning impossible.'

Taking a wide guess, the independent House of Commons Library is predicting that by 2056 there will be an extra 17 million people living in England, which would push the total to somewhere between 70 and 80 million, not counting 'short-term' migrants.

Prior to the 'downturn', the average family paid a lifetime's tax bill of £668,000, according to the TaxPayers' Alliance. With public borrowing too huge to grasp, the figure is expected to soar dramatically in coming years.

'The government say they sympathise with the plight of ordinary people, but they don't seem to care about the massive tax burden that people have to pay throughout their lives,' says the group's research director, Corin Taylor.

In another poll, the group found that 64 percent believed the government was taxing and spending too much and 74 percent accused politicians of using environmental concerns as an excuse to bring in green taxes. Overall, people feel the government is no longer working in their best interests.

Ann Robinson, director of consumer policy at uSwitch.com, says we are getting a raw deal from the government for the fruits of our labour and says when it comes to quality of life, we remain the 'sick man of Europe'.

STATE OF HEALTH

Today there are more doctors and nurses than ever before. New hospitals are being built, mortality rates for cancer and heart disease are falling and patient satisfaction is high' – Alan Johnson, Secretary of State for Health (2007-2009).

ONE-in-four cancer patients are denied treatment on grounds of cost, according to one cancer charity, with more than 1,300 patients across the country being 'left to die' if their local trusts refuse to fund treatment.

These drugs are widely available throughout Western Europe and in some cases in Scotland, says the charity Rarer Cancers Forum (RCF) which obtained the figures under the Freedom of Information Act.

And it says patients in England and Wales are effectively being 'left to die' if they fail to persuade their local trusts to fund treatment.

NHS trusts have a legal obligation to provide treatments approved by the National Institute for Health and Clinical Excellence (Nice), which assesses the cost-effectiveness of new medicines in England and Wales.

If the drug is not on the approved list, the patient must appeal to a committee at the local trust, which can choose to fund it as an 'exceptional' case. Those who are refused must settle for a less effective treatment or pay privately.

The charity says the released figures show widespread regional variations in the chances of being granted access to these drugs. Of 25 patients living in Mid Essex who applied for non-approved treatment, only one had a request rejected, while all three patients who made requests in neighbouring South West Essex were turned down.

Penny Wilson-Webb, chief executive of the RCF, says the approvals procedure is often chaotic and varies widely across the country, with patients being forced to 'plead for their lives'.

'These life-and-death judgments are made behind closed doors by secretive 'priorities panels' dominated by NHS managers,' says the charity. 'With each panel reaching their decisions in a different way, the report shows a striking postcode lottery in the chances of having an 'exceptional request' approved.'

Turning down the beds

BRITAIN now has 32,000 less NHS hospital beds than it did when New Labour came to power despite a dramatic rise in the population. Government figures show beds are being reduced at an alarming rate which patients' groups describe as 'a national scandal'.

The figures show that NHS hospitals had just over 167,000 beds in 2007 compared with 199,000 in 1997. Numbers fell dramatically in 2007, despite fears that overcrowding leads to a higher risk of superbug infections.

More than 8,450 beds were lost in the year ending March 2007, the biggest cut in 14 years. Tory health spokesman Andrew Lansley described the cuts as 'potentially life-threatening'.

'The government's approach of care closer to home and cutting beds can only work if there is the investment in high quality community services,' he says. 'But it's just not happening. Hospital admissions and emergency attendances remain high.'

However, the government insists that the fall in hospital beds is a sign of a healthy NHS. 'General and acute bed numbers are decreasing because hospitals are dealing with patients more efficiently,' said a Health Department spokesperson.

Agony over targets

PATIENTS are being discharged from accident and emergency departments before they have been properly treated in order to meet government targets and those waiting to be treated are waiting longer – often in agony – says the British Medical Association.

The BMA says injuries are not given the fullest treatment because of a government diktat to either find patients a bed within four hours or discharge them.

And it says people needing urgent surgery are being forced to endure agonising waits rather than receive treatment ahead of more routine cases because if they are fast-tracked, hospitals could miss a second target, which is to treat all patients referred by a GP within 18 weeks.

Doctors say pressure on beds means patients needing urgent care are being sent home so that hospitals are not penalised for exceeding the four-hour A&E target. Others are being treated in ambulances 'stacked' outside A&E departments, so the clock measuring the time people wait in casualty units does not start ticking.

Surgeons say the pressure to meet targets means they cannot prioritise the most pressing cases, with many patients suffering because they are forced to the back of the queue.

Almost 17,000 operations were cancelled in the first quarter of 2008 – twice as many as the same period the previous year.

John Carvell of the BMA says: 'We are concerned that this trend is going to keep getting worse and …we are going to see waiting targets coming down further and further, distorting clinical decisions which need to be made by doctors.'

The situation has deteriorated so rapidly says a report by the NHS Confederation that nurses and doctors do not have the time for compassion and it says the need to meet budgets means the more humane aspects of health care – diet, pain control and hygiene – are now sidelined.

Failure to provide humane care has become endemic in the health services because beleaguered staff have too little time to pay adequate attention to fundamental human needs, the body adds.

'The most shocking thing is that these basic failings are the rule rather than the exception. Compassion as a concept is largely missing from health policy,' says the report's author, Dr Robin Youngson.

Bribing down budgets

DOCTORS are being paid cash bonuses not to refer patients for treatment in hospital. Under the controversial scheme branded by some as 'dangerous' the average surgery of 10,000 patients can earn an extra £20,000 a year while saving local health authorities millions of pounds.

In Oxfordshire, the Primary Care Trust is paying GPs £1 per patient if they reconsider a decision to send someone to hospital. They also receive a separate bonus for cutting referral rates.

The scheme's introduction in England and Wales coincided with a government admission that the average GP now earns over £100,000 a year while two-thirds of patients must wait more than two days for an appointment.

The bonus money is paid directly into accounts of the practice along with salaries and is seen as a direct financial incentive to refuse further treatment for patients.

'I don't think patients' services should be treated as a commodity,' says Laurence Buckman, chairman of the British Medical Association's GP Committee, explaining: 'A large number of patients are referred to hospital for investigation. If you don't know what's wrong, you cannot know how to handle the problem.'

Primary Health Trusts across the country have seen an unexplained rise in the number of hospital referrals in recent years and see the scheme as a good way of halting the trend.

'Financial incentives to encourage GPs to reduce referral rates can be effective,' says the National Institute for Health Research. 'But this is a high risk.'

Sue Woollacott, chairman of an Oxford patient support group, goes a little further: 'If I were a GP and getting payments for the practice, it would seem like some sort of bribe.'

The lost principles

A FIXATION with bureaucracy and budgets has pushed the

National Health Service towards 'catastrophic meltdown' says a senior doctor who believes the government's obsession with red tape and political correctness results in dire care for patients.

Professor Paul Goddard, former president of the Royal Society of Medicine, also slammed Nice for putting budgets before people.

'If they think a patient will gain an extra year of life – but it will cost more than £20,000 – they think it's not cost-effective,' says the professor who quit the NHS saying the government had lost sight of the basic principles of a national health service.

'The NHS was built on the foundation of caring for the community. It was designed to help those who needed help, care for those who needed care and treat those who needed treatment,' he says.

'Those basic principles have been lost as the government takes us down a dangerous path that can only be a catastrophic meltdown of the system.'

The poor die young

BRITAIN'S poorer families are dying younger than their European counterparts says the World Health Organisation. Low incomes, poor education, bad housing and a failure to curb junk food and adopt healthy transport policies are all contributory factors says the UN body.

The report – produced by British professor Sir Michael Marmot – shows that the ill-health and shorter lives of those on low incomes has brought down life expectancy to just 79 years. Japan, Australia, Sweden, Canada and Italy all have an average of 83 years.

'Social injustice is killing people on a grand scale,' claims the WHO.

The report shows harsh disparities within the UK. A boy from the Glasgow suburb of Calton can expect to live 28 years less than one from neighbouring Lenzie. And a boy in London's desirable Hampstead will live 11 years longer than one from down-market St Pancras.

If they live

BRITISH babies are less likely to survive their first year than those of neighbouring countries says the government's own Office for National Statistics – with infant death rates for the UK among the worst in Europe.

Britain comes in at 18th position in a European table of child mortality – behind former communist nations like the Czech Republic and Slovenia.

The ONS study showed 5.1 children in every 1,000 died before their first birthday in 2005. In contrast, child mortality in Greece dropped from 5.1 in 2002 to 3.8 in 2005.

Child mortality is considered one of the key measures of national wealth and well-being.

ED ED ED

'Ask me my three main priorities for government, and I tell you: education, education, education' – Tony Blair.

ELEVEN years after the famous rallying call to supporters at the 1996 party conference official figures show that Britain's school children could do a lot better. They could also be better served.

Britain squeezes more primary school children into its classes than almost any other developed country says the Organisation for Economic Co-operation and Development (OECD). It also says fewer students are graduating in Britain than before.

UK State primaries have 24.5 pupils per class – the fourth largest of the 30 Western countries which make up the OECD.

Only Japan, Korea and Turkey have more crowded primary classrooms.

The gap between private and State school class sizes is higher in the UK than in any other country with on average 13 more pupils in a state primary class than in a private one. In other OECD countries, private and state schools have similar class sizes.

It says Britain is slipping down the chart with fewer young people graduating from university. In 2000, the UK had the fourth highest graduation rate of the OECD. Today, the UK is struggling to keep pace and has dropped to 12th place.

One in seven primary school children has difficulty writing their name at the end of their first year says the Department for Children, Schools and Families. Some 14 percent of five-year-olds cannot spell 'mum' or their own first name.

The figures show 11 percent cannot remember the alphabet while four primary school children in ten cannot write a simple letter to Father Christmas. Only half the children assessed are said to have reached a 'good level of development'.

Government guidelines say five-year-olds have reached a 'good level' when they can concentrate, understand school rules, join in conversations; and understand simple sentences. They must also demonstrate that they 'respect' others.

Older children fair little better. Among 14-year-old boys, one in five has a reading age of nine while an entire third have reading ages of 11 or lower, according to national test results.

Boys have seen their reading skills drop dramatically under the government's education policies, with 36 percent failing in their SATs tests. The figures show an alarming decline the longer boys spend at school. One-sixth of those tested scored lower marks after three years in secondary school than they did in their final year at primary.

Ministers have been quick to blame parents for the rapid drop-off in standards, with Schools Minister Jim Knight saying they must limit time spent on-line and on computer games and encourage boys to read more books at home instead of watching television.

But parents question where the additional money spent on education has gone. Although the budget has doubled over the past decade to £63.7 billion a year, examiners say 15 percent of boys failed to even register a score in tests, while six per cent were considered so far from the required standard that they were not even entered. Two per cent were absent on test days.

WUT U doin englsh 4?

WITH English taking a back seat, the pass rate for GCSE exams soared to an amazing 98.4 percent in 2008. More than a fifth of pupils were awarded grade A passes or higher. Ministers were quick to laud success in such diverse subjects as the Expressive Arts, Media Studies, and Statistics.

Results for English were not so good with examiners noting a 'decline in technical accuracy'. Fortunately, with the emphasis now on 'expression', spelling, punctuation and grammar only account for about 13 percent of the marks

'While the correct use of the apostrophe continues to grow, the use of the comma declines,' says the Assessment and Qualifications Alliance. 'A high percentage of scripts [exam papers] did not involve a single comma. The semi-colon is making an attempt at re-appearance, sometimes used correctly.'

In a report detailing the declining standards in written English, the Alliance says: 'Misuse of there/they're, your/you're, been/being, of/have were relatively widespread and there was a noted increase in the text version U.'

Professor Alan Smithers, director of the Centre for Education and Employment Research at Buckingham University, says children should have learnt the difference between 'they're' and 'there' in primary school or by the early years of secondary at the latest.

He says schools have neglected 'important things like being

able to spell and punctuate properly' in favour of 'more creative things like empathising and drama and so on'.

'We are now discovering that children don't just pick up these things. It depends on a lot of hard work that the school curriculum has to encourage,' he says.

With attention spans wavering, it is now possible to score full marks in English Literature without ever having picked up a book. With only extracts to go by, many pupils believe *Romeo and Juliet* has a happy ending.

Critics say exam boards and the government's curriculum advisers, the Qualifications and Curriculum Authority, have caved in to the sound-bite society by encouraging teachers to concentrate on bite-sized chunks of text instead of the full novel, play or poem.

'It is now possible to complete an entire secondary school education without ever having read a book cover-to-cover,' insists Anthony Farrell, the head of English at St Ives School in Cornwall, who says the cult of extracts has replaced reading for pleasure.

In a report co-authored with Professor David Jesson of York University, they say English literature has turned into a comprehension exercise with 'self-contained chunks of texts reproduced in exam papers on which pupils can answer questions without the need to show an understanding of the whole work or its genre'.

They claim a target-driven education policy is silencing pupils' voices and creative instincts, with teachers encouraged by the 'assessment-led and data-driven regime' to drill their pupils to perform well in exams. The pleasure of reading has been forgotten.

'There's no time for that because of the reductive exam syllabuses and pressure to get results,' says the report.

Help for the hapless

THE focus on emotional expression over educational knowledge is 'infantilising' students and setting them up for a fall in later life say two Oxford academics.

'Turning teaching into therapy is destroying the minds of children, young people and adults,' insists Dr Dennis Hayes. 'Therapeutic education promotes the idea that we are emotional, vulnerable and hapless individuals. It is an attack on human potential.'

In their book *The Dangerous Rise of Therapeutic Education*, they criticise the recent introduction into State schools of lessons in happiness and wellbeing under a programme known as Social and Emotional Aspects of Learning – SEAL for short.

'Everyone looks for a difficulty to declare, like the hundreds of students who register themselves as dyslexic. Being dyslexic used to be something that people hid. Now students wear their difficulties as a badge of honour,' Dr Hayes said.

Government guidelines say teaching children to express their emotions boosts concentration and motivation.

Co-author Frank Furedi, Professor of Sociology at the University of Kent, says: 'It inflates the importance of feelings to the point where they eclipse what is supposed to be going on in the classroom.'

He says it also makes teachers and lecturers overcautious. 'They will give a piece of work 55 percent and then write on it 'this essay is superb' because they daren't say it's crap.'

Oral stress

THE government's Qualifications and Curriculum Authority says children learning foreign languages should not be tested on their ability to speak the language because the stress involved puts pupils off learning.

The recommendations by Lord Dearing – which were accepted by then-Education Secretary Alan Johnson in March 2007 – were immediately branded 'stupid' by the former chief inspector of schools, Chris Woodhead.

'It's stupid because if one is wanting to know if someone has mastered a foreign language in any context, then clearly the student has got to be able to speak that language in any context,' he said.

Fewer pupils are taking foreign language GCSEs. A study of 1,000 schools in England and Wales saw a 30 percent slump in the number of pupils studying modern languages since the government dropped compulsory language courses in 2003.

Don't use the S-word

EDUCATION experts say many children are being put off learning because the word 'school' is too intimidating and not sufficiently 'inclusive' and they want to see Britain's education establishments re-branded as 'places of learning'.

Barnsley has already dropped the words 'secondary school' and replaced them with 'advanced learning centres' under the 'Remaking Learning' programme that hopes to 'regenerate' the community by 'embracing all ages of learning'.

The Watercliffe Meadow Primary in Sheffield dropped the s-word to soften its image. 'One reason was many of the parents of the children here had very negative connotations of school,' explained head teacher Linda Kingdon.

'Instead, we want this to be a place for family learning, where anyone can come. We wanted to deinstitutionalise the place and bring the school closer to real life.'

Such talk is twaddle insists local MP, Richard Caborn. 'I'm always open to new ideas but the reality is education is about preparing young people to live in the real world.'

Hundreds of secondary schools have recently re-branded themselves as colleges in a bid to improve their image. But such moves are meaningless says Professor Alan Smithers of the University of Buckingham.

'Frankly, calling something a learning centre is likely to confuse parents and it rather diminishes the institution,' he says.

The lost generation

GOVERNMENT obsession with targets and pass rates has condemned almost four million children to dead-end jobs at the cost of £70 billion of wasted taxpayers' money says the Bow Group think-tank.

After more than a decade of New Labour, more teenagers are leaving school without even the most basic qualifications. Official figures show that fewer than half of all teenagers finish compulsory schooling with a basic set of GCSE qualifications while one-in-five fails to gain a single C grade.

Results for the first pupils to go through their entire education under New Labour show that more than 340,000 16-year-olds failed to meet the government's secondary school benchmark of five C grade GCSEs or higher, including English and maths.

More than 135,000 failed to achieve even one C grade in 2008.

The Bow Group says official figures fail to show a 'lost generation' hidden at the bottom of the pile.

The report, *The Failed Generation – the real cost of education under Labour*, shows that in 2007 nearly one in six pupils failed to get five GCSEs of any grade – the worst results in 10 years.

'These pupils were five when Labour came to power. There are simply no more excuses for this level of persistent and sustained record of failure,' says Chris Skidmore, chairman of the Bow Group and author of the report. 'We have witnessed a decade of disappointment in which an entire generation of pupils have been let down.'

A survey by the Learning and Skills Council shows that over 20 percent of employers would not hire teenagers without the grades or a vocational equivalent. Some 15 percent said they would ignore applications completely.

The Bow report shows spending on each pupil has risen dramatically from £2,910 in 1997 to £5,080 in 2007. It estimates that £70 billion has been wasted on children destined to fail within the current system.

'You could say that the system is wasting taxpayers' money because we are giving these children the wrong type of education,' says Margaret Morrissey of the National Confederation of Parent Teacher Associations.

'If they were not going to achieve those grades, why did we try to make them?' she asks. 'Shouldn't we be providing an alternative for youngsters so they can come out of school with useful qualifications and a little bit of self-esteem?'

PUTTING THE CUSTOMER FIRST

'We are not just a brand, we are an institution. We have the trust of the nation and we can't let them down because we are The People's Post Office' – television commercial.

IT'S ALL so cosy: a nice little corner Post Office and a bumbling manager talking about the trust of the nation while *Land of Hope and Glory* plays in the background. But the multi-million-pound ad campaign had customers screaming hypocrisy at a time when the government was closing 2,500 post offices.

'Is this some kind of sick joke?' asked one of seemingly millions of people blogging on the subject of Post Office closures.

The Post Office believe the 2007-2008 commercials – featuring lovable household names such as Bill Oddie and Keith Harris and Orville – warmed the public towards the brand. It was also intended to boost fortunes at a time when the government was taking traditional services out of Post Offices and into the hands of big business.

Many people see more than simple hypocracy in the campaign. There are accusations of deliberate deception.

'They have kept the truth about how they are carrying out the closure programme from the general public,' says the Campaign Against Post Office Closures. 'The population at large still believe that only unviable Post Offices are being closed – not only is this not true, Post Office Ltd are leaving little used unviable Post Offices open.'

Jenny Wright thought her eyes were deceiving her when she stumbled on the actual Post Office used in the commercials just yards from her home in Richmond on the outskirts of London. It had previously been a derelict lighting and bathroom shop. Her actual Post Office, just 300 yards down the road, had been controversially closed shortly before filming.

'I was absolutely astonished to see it disguised as a Post Office,' she said.

The decision to film in the town provoked an outcry. Liberal Democrat MP Susan Kramer accused Post Office bosses of 'despicable behaviour'. She said: 'As a result of their closure programme, Richmond town centre has only one Post Office left – and that's on the first floor of WH Smith.

'They should have spent the money on reopening the sub-Post Office which was heavily used, particularly by old people. This adds insult to injury.'

The government as the sole share-holder of the Post Office has been accused of destroying a 350-year-old institution, and of selling off its profitable services to the private sector.

The cuts have been felt hardest in rural communities which have already seen their shops, banks and pubs close, along with schools, police stations and hospitals. For many, the closure of their Post Office is the final nail in the coffin.

In Brompton Regis, postmaster Peter Stringer said the closure also means the end of the village stores which he runs with his wife Jenny. 'It will be the death of the shop because the shop cannot stand alone with the loss of income from the full-time Post Office. They are ripping the heart out of this community for the sake of a few thousand pounds a year.'

Campaigners believe the next target will be the Royal Mail's universal service, the obligation to provide a 'one-price-goes-anywhere' distribution of letters and parcels to all locations across the UK.

'And it's not just private correspondence that would suffer if the universal service were stopped,' warns Jeff Randall in the *Daily Telegraph*. 'Many small businesses in remote areas are wholly reliant on Royal Mail. Don't talk to them about alternative carriers, there aren't any.'

The Communication Workers Union (CWU) criticised what it said was a 'competition at all costs' ethos which puts the Post Office at a serious competitive disadvantage to its European rivals. It says the regulator has moved in a way that is 'completely out of step with the carefully managed approach' set out in European legislation.

'In so doing, Postcomm has placed significant extra pressures on the Royal Mail Group at a time when it is undergoing far-reaching internal and external changes,' said CWU deputy general secretary Dave Ward. 'The upshot will be to place very real pressures on Royal Mail's ability to meet its universal service obligations.'

Campaigners hoping to halt the Post Office closures by citing the government's obligations under its own Disability Equality Duty (DED) were stunned to discover that they had been pipped at the post.

Around 45,000 public bodies are covered by the DED which is meant to ensure they pay 'due regard' to the promotion of equality for disabled people in every area of operation. This includes local access to a Post Office.

But the man overseeing the closure programme – Business Secretary John Hutton – cynically exempted Royal Mail from the DED shortly before announcing the cuts.

Campaigner Jonathan Coe, whose wife is disabled, described the government's callous disregard of its own rules as an outrage.

'Neither the government nor the Post Office seem to

understand why retaining local Post Offices is so important to those who are disabled and elderly, particularly those on low incomes and those who do not have access to cars and to the internet.'

'Our local Post Office is being closed even though it is used by over 1,000 people a week and makes a profit.'

HONOURING OUR ELDERS

'Tackling pensioner poverty is a priority' – Mike O'Brien, Secretary of State for Work and Pensions [2007-2008].

MORE old people are filling our prisons than ever before. The number of men over 60 incarcerated is up 34 percent with women over 50 increasing by 40 percent, so says Anne Owers, HM Chief Inspector of Prisons. And nobody wants to explain why.

She says the proportion of older prisoners previously hovered around 2.4 percent for men and 6 percent for women. But in 2007 the figures suddenly jumped sharply.

It was not in Miss Owers' remit to question why so many more pensioners are being sent to prison, although one explanation is that more people are being locked up today – contrary to popular belief – and are receiving longer sentences. People, including prisoners, are also living longer.

Many prisoners are also aging inside their jails. It is thought that 20 percent of the over 60 prison population are serving life sentences.

'Older prisoners still face the double punishment of being locked up in prisons that take little or no account of the needs of the elderly,' says Juliet Lyon, director of the Prison Reform Trust. 'An ageing prison population is being squeezed into overcrowded jails designed and run for young men.'

According to David Howarth, the Liberal Democrats' justice spokesman: 'This is yet another example of ministers not thinking through the long term consequences of their short term political fixes.'

The Ministry of Justice declined to comment on the sudden increase in pensioners behind bars.

Taking a stand

RICHARD Fitzmaurice is a convicted criminal who has served time. He is also a 76-year-old former soldier who once proudly served his country. But he was led away in handcuffs to join a growing band of pensioners filling our prisons. Former Warrant Officer Fitzmaurice withheld some of his council tax.

He describes his long-running feud with King's Lynn and West Norfolk Borough Council as a battle on behalf of struggling pensioners who can no longer afford to pay crippling council charges.

'I'm not doing this for me specifically,' he insists. 'There are many old-age pensioners who are not as well off as I am who cannot keep facing these increases.'

Mr Fitzmaurice served three days of his 34-day sentence for 'wilful refusal' to pay before his family quietly paid the fine on his behalf.

Rising council taxes – which often represent a third of a pensioner's total income – are blamed for the dramatic increase in the number of elderly people in poverty. Their numbers jumped by an additional 300,000 in 2008 to bring 2.5 million to the depths of despair.

Pension's minister at the time, Mike O'Brien, admitted one of the 'key explanations' for the rise was the decision in 2006 not to renew a £200 council tax rebate for the elderly.

More than 60 percent of single pensioners have to survive on less than £200 a week, according to the Office for National

Statistics. Around 60 percent of single pensioners receive less than £10,000 a year and 45 percent of pensioner couples are on less than £15,000 at a time of spiralling prices.

'The government should be mortified by the latest rise in pensioner poverty,' says Mervyn Kohler, a special adviser for Help the Aged, who says the numbers represent 822 pensioners falling into the poverty trap every single day.

'When older people live on a fixed income it's virtually impossible for them to pull themselves out of poverty. Pensioners often have to cut back on essential household items just to survive,' he explained. 'This is a disgrace.'

According to insurance giant Prudential, more than a million pensioners have an average debt of £15,500, and as many as 70,000 retirees have debts of between £50,000 and £75,000. Ray Sprigg, a money adviser for Help the Aged, says more and more pensioners are confused by modern money markets and are desperate for advice.

'The present generation of older people have lived through a period of massive change in money management thinking – while bankruptcy used to be an exception among older people they are now very much the norm with our clients,' he said.

'Stress and shame associated with debt seems to affect older people far more than our younger clients,' he said, adding: 'Credit collection agencies and threats from bailiffs often cause genuine worry and illness.'

When Moses Adegoke could not find the money to pay his full council tax demand the bailiffs were quick to step in.

'They were calling me on my mobile phone and landline and really made my life hell,' said Mr Adegoke, 61, a diabetic dependent on insulin who also suffers from severe hypertension. His home was then bombarded with threatening letters.

In order to meet the £800 bill – including additional collection charges – bailiffs Rundle & Co wrote to say: 'I will be calling, with transportation, to remove your goods during the course of this coming week. Goods will be removed whether you are present or not, with the police in attendance if necessary.'

'I was terrified and thought they were coming to break into my house and take everything I owned,' said Mr Adegoke. 'My blood pressure shot up and I couldn't sleep, I was so worried. I wanted to end it all.'

Thanet Council in Kent were accused of pushing a 91-year-old widow to the depths of despair when they sent her bills totalling £16,000 to make her former council home 'eco-friendly'.

Bed-ridden Dorothy Hacking was 'petrified' of eviction if she did not pay the bill for external cladding work at her home in Ramsgate. She was forced to re-mortgage to find the extra £112 a month to pay her debts.

'It's disgusting she was faced with this fear when the council insisted on doing work over which she had no control,' said her daughter, Rosemary Brown, an English teacher at Margate's Kent Adult Education Centre.

'She was financially stretched to the limit, worried about putting the heating on in case she couldn't pay the bills and had no idea what to do if another big bill arrived from the council,' she told the *Thanet Gazette*.

Eight years earlier, she had been forced to borrow £6,500 for balcony repairs and feared that further repairs to sewers could run to thousands of pounds. Her local paper launched a front-page appeal to help the pensioner.

'Sadly my mum died on the day of publication. She didn't see the article because she was too weak that day. But hopefully it will help to raise awareness of what the council is continuing to do,' said Mrs Brown.

Thanet councillor Zita Wiltshire said Mrs Hacking had been consulted over the cladding charges in 2006.

'We are sympathetic to the concerns of our leaseholders but the council does spell out the detail of the financial obligations imposed upon a lessee in the terms of each right-to-buy lease,' she explained.

Under the Home Energy Conservation Act, councils are

obliged to reduce CO_2 emissions by 30 percent over 10 years.

Another former serviceman – great-grandfather Walter Bargate – tried to take his life when an inflated electricity bill tipped him beyond desperation. It later transpired that the company E.ON had incorrectly installed the meter, doubling his bills.

After visits from threatening bailiffs, the vulnerable pensioner – who served in the RAF in the Second World War – swallowed 100 pills and tried to end it all.

Mr Bargate, 84, left a heartbreaking note to his children – scrawled in the darkness of his blacked out home – naming the firm as the 'catalyst' for his suicide attempt.

'It chokes me to think how desperate he must have felt,' said his daughter, Sarah Hayes. 'They behaved in the most atrocious manner from beginning to end. I'm disgusted with this company, who even a few days before my father's suicide attempt could not recognise his vulnerability.'

Watchdog Energywatch blamed E.ON for a 'catalogue of crass errors' and said vulnerable customers needed extra protection at a time when energy bills are soaring.

Treasury's OAP windfall

THE government hopes to save £301 million over two years by cutting backdated welfare payments to Britain's poorest pensioners. Those who fail to claim their full entitlement to pension credit – and the associated housing and council tax benefit – will only get three months' worth of reimbursements rather than a full year.

'Reducing the amount of backdated pension credit, housing benefit and council tax benefit older people can receive to just three months will penalise some of the poorest pensioners,' says Gordon Lishman, director general of Age Concern, who says many old people are simply confused by the system.

The figures, which were not made available to Parliament or

the public, were uncovered by Liberal Democrat MP Lynne Featherstone, who described the cost-cutting measure as 'the worst kind of Labour penny-pinching'.

'The Treasury is in for a real windfall at the expense of some of the poorest people in the country,' she says. 'Pensioners on fixed incomes are bearing the brunt of bumper rises in fuel and shopping bills. It's outrageous that the government has targeted them to claw back millions of pounds.'

Pension credit was introduced in 2003 and represents a vital top-up for pensioners who would otherwise be living below the breadline. But Age Concern says six in 10 pensioners are put off claiming the money because of complicated forms and the associated shame of means testing.

The backdating of pension credit will save the Treasury £100 million in 2009 and £96 million in 2010. Similar reforms of housing and council tax benefit will save £35 million in 2009 and £70 million in 2010.

Savings plundered

A TREASURY blunder which left £135 million in taxes uncollected every year for the past 25 years is now being clawed back from hard-pressed pensioners.

More than 420,000 pensioners are being forced to pay tax on their life's savings, with each facing bills averaging £320 a year until the £3.3 billion is paid back.

Ministers admitted the extra bills could place some pensioners 'in difficulty' after a damning report by the National Audit Office on HM Revenue and Customs' accounts.

The Revenue began deducting the unpaid tax from pensions at source in April 2009, to a muted public outcry.

'Not content with letting the State pension fall behind the cost of living they are now trying to whittle down private pension saving too,' said Liberal Democrat work and pensions spokeswoman Jenny Willott.

'It's unacceptable that HMRC blunders should leave pensioners facing a higher tax bill. It's a tax grab by anyone's standards.'

Pensions 'sexist'

ONE IN four of all female pensioners are living in poverty because the State pension discriminates against women, says Age Concern and the equal rights organisation the Fawcett Society.

They say women receive pensions far lower than men, with the pay gap between men and women during their working lives becoming a vast 'pension gulf' in later life.

The report found that women got just 32p for every £1 of income received by men in a pensioner couple.

'The current State pension system is not working for women as it is based on the old assumption of men as the breadwinners and women as stay-at-home carers,' says Katherine Rake, director of the Fawcett Society.

Rock on

BRITAIN'S aging population may have to fend for itself with local authorities woefully ill-prepared to cope with the next generation of old folk.

The Audit Commission says 27 percent of town halls have no strategy and almost half were only starting to develop ideas.

The Local Government Association is worried that with 40 percent of the population topping 50 in a few years time it will be unable to cope with their specific wants and needs.

'Ex-punk rockers and Rolling Stones fans are not going to be happy with a cup of tea and daytime TV,' says Commission chairman Michael O'Higgins.

'Despite the stereotypes, only 3 percent of people aged between 65 and 80 live in residential care,' he says. 'But it's worrying that the councils in areas with the most over-50s are the least prepared to cope with their long-term needs and interests.'

The report suggests councils find ways of helping the 'new oldies' stay well and independent, and cites as examples a council-funded community radio station for retirees in rural Cornwall and an awareness scheme to prevent trips and falls in the West Midlands that saved millions of pounds in hip operations.

THE COVENANT OF CARE

'Britain has a duty of care to its armed forces. This began as an unspoken pact between society and the military, possibly originating as far back as Henry VIII's reign. The pact was formally codified as a 'covenant' in 2000. It is not a law but is reinforced by custom and convention' – Army Doctrine Publication Volume 5

SOLDIERS returning from Britain's wars in Iraq and Afghanistan are being sent to prison in increasing numbers. Charities blame their intensified training and exposure to real-life horrors for their acts of violence when they come home and say the military is simply dumping 'ticking time bombs' onto the streets – and into prisons.

Home Office figures show at least 8,500 former soldiers are in custody – 9 percent of the UK prison population and nearly double the estimate of the previous study in 2004.

They form the largest single group by profession in the prison system. And the true figure is thought to be considerably higher.

The Justice Department has issued no guidelines to courts on how to deal with veterans up before the bench, although it does acknowledge some of the problems returning soldiers face. An internal report cites the example of one 23-year-old para and his difficulty readjusting after two active tours of duty.

'He found it hard to reconcile the devastation, horror and

distress of the war zone with the comfortable life he found himself and others taking for granted,' said the report.

'He self-medicated over a number of years using alcohol, became aggressive towards partners and others, and is currently serving four months for assault.'

Despite the ministry being aware of his case, the former soldier who answered his country's call has received five custodial sentences since leaving the Parachute Regiment in late 2005.

Jimmy Johnson speaks out on the issue for the organisation Veterans in Prison.

'Since the end of the Second World War, the MoD have been in pursuit of creating professional 'super soldiers' who will kill other human beings with no hesitation or conscience.'

But he says the military does virtually nothing to help these men readjust to civilian life. 'With troops left brainwashed and switched-on to violence, they are left with a sort of Dr Jekyll and Mr Hyde syndrome – Dr Jekyll comes home from the wars and brings Mr Hyde with him.'

One MP became concerned when he noticed ex-servicemen being sentenced in north Wales courts for assault with worrying regularity. Plaid Cymru MP Elfyn Llwyd says the government has let these men down because there is no help for them.

'I have come to the conclusion that if proper treatment was available for these disturbed servicemen, hundreds if not thousands would not have offended,' he says. 'The government is letting them and their families down very badly indeed.'

Harry Fletcher, assistant general secretary of Napo – representing probation and family court staff – believes the official figures do not represent the growing numbers of servicemen in jail and says the vast majority of offences are violent and related to drugs or alcohol.

'There is no systematic availability of stress-related counselling. This should be made available without delay and would drastically reduce the number of receptions into custody.'

Best-selling author Andy McNab has seen two of his former

SAS colleagues commit suicide while a third shot his girlfriend dead. He says care is 'totally inadequate' and that the NHS has been woefully ill-prepared for the influx of returning troops – an estimated 15 percent of whom go on to suffer from post-traumatic stress disorder (PTSD).

'I've seen for myself the appalling way that our soldiers are hung out to dry,' he says. 'The idea held by the government that the majority of service personnel experience a smooth transition into civilian life is delusional and largely false.'

'The number of soldiers in prison is definitely on the rise,' insists Tracey Johnson of Veterans in Prison. 'They're fighting in back-to-back conflicts, coming out and going back again. They haven't got time to recover. There are not enough of them. They don't have the right cover or equipment and they're absolutely knackered.'

Her organisation has been swamped with letters from soldiers in prison. In virtually every case she believes the writers were suffering from PTSD. She gives the example of a letter from one man whose son was jailed for threatening to shoot another soldier.

'He had been wetting his bed and in floods of tears because he couldn't get Iraq out of his head.'

'We only had a 10-20 minute presentation on PTSD at Basra airport,' said a Sergeant Major who served over 20 years in the Territorials. 'It was given at 11.30 pm at night when we were absolutely fragged and we had been through a real nightmare. I was sent home with no counselling or decompression talk.'

'He had a breakdown and was eventually diagnosed as suffering combat related PTSD,' says Jimmy Johnson.

'Before these men stepped forward and volunteered to defend their country, not one of them had served a prison sentence,' he points out. 'But on their return from war they have become a higher percentage rate than any other profession in the entire prison population.'

'These are the casualties that should never have been,' he says.

'Help for heroes'

IT TOOK a lot of bad publicity before the MoD dug a little deeper into its coffers to help Lance-Bombardier Ben Parkinson. Although doctors described him as 'Britain's worst-wounded soldier', strict rules meant he could only claim for three of his 37 injuries. His family were mortified when he was offered around half the available compensation.

The 23-year-old lost both his legs when he was blown up by a landmine in Afghanistan. He also sustained grievous damage to his spine, skull, pelvis, hands, spleen and ribcage. Only major advances in battlefield surgery kept him alive and doctors say he would certainly have died of his injuries in any previous war.

When the letter from the MoD arrived, few expected that he would be offered a paltry pay-out of £152,150. His parents contacted their local paper, *Doncaster Today*, which took up the fight and soon the nationals were on the case.

They highlighted Ben's appalling injuries and ruined life and compared how the MoD compensated one of its own civil servants with £202,000 for back strain after lifting a printer. Then there was the £217,000 payout to another civil servant with depression, and even a Forces typist who got £485,000 for hurting her thumb.

In the end, Defence Secretary Des Browne caved in to public outrage and announced the MoD would bump up Ben's compensation to £285,00, which he described as 'generous'. Ben's parents, however, were said to be 'disappointed'.

His mother, Diane Dernie of Doncaster, South Yorkshire, said the extra money would help get Ben set up but she described it as the 'bare minimum'.

'It's still nowhere near enough to give him the kind of security he needs or cope with extra expenses.'

Although she had nothing but praise for Ben's medical treatment, she is bitter at a government which she says treats wounded soldiers as a 'commodity'.

'They are simply figures on a balance sheet. They do not have any role, any function and the MoD wants to dispose of them as cheaply as possible.'

Her views on an uncaring government are shared by hundreds of other military families who feel cheated and say the additional pay-outs granted by the ministry are paltry.

When Sergeant Steven Llewelyn's ambulance was shot up and looted by criminals in southern Iraq he was left 40 percent disabled. His first appeal for compensation was turned down and then he discovered that he was no longer entitled to put in another claim.

As his vehicle had been attacked by 'civilians', he was first advised to claim under the MoD's criminal injuries compensation overseas scheme, where frontline troops can claim for injury or death 'not caused by military operations against the Taliban or Iraqi militia' and receive up to £500,000.

His claim was rejected because the MoD did not agree who carried out the attack. The 45-year-old, who was subsequently medically discharged from the Army, says: 'Men have been sent to Iraq, their friends have died and they are getting nothing. It's absolutely disgraceful.'

Lawyers say an increasing number of injured frontline troops are being denied their rightful compensation, often on what might be seen as trifling technicalities.

In Afghanistan – where the Soviet legacy has left an estimated 50 million unexploded landmines and other active ordinance – British forces are finding they could step on the wrong kind of bomb and miss out on compensation.

More often than not, the MoD refuses to accept that these weapons have been left behind from the earlier conflict and claims instead that they were deliberately planted by the enemy to target British troops, thereby lowering any potential pay-out.

'The government's logic is bizarre and they are clearly wriggling out of paying men injured in war zones by suggesting they have been injured by the wrong type of bomb,' says solicitor Hilary Meredith.

The actual scale of injuries according to soldiers, MPs and lawyers representing injured servicemen and women is being hidden from the public for political reasons.

A *Sunday Telegraph* report showed that every week dozens of soldiers are being injured, some severely, yet details of the nature and severity of the wounds are never made public.

'While the Ministry of Defence argues that details of injuries are not released to protect the soldiers' families from media intrusion, many within the military believe the policy is designed to keep secret the attrition rate being suffered by the Army in Afghanistan,' says the paper.

Darren Fuller joined the Army at 17. By 31 he was a sergeant serving with the Second Battalion the Parachute Regiment in Helmand Province. And then his arm was blown off by a faulty mortar round.

'I ducked down as the bomb fired out and then I saw that my hand, wrist and about half of my forearm had disappeared,' he recounts. 'It was a complete mess. I didn't think something like this would happen to me.'

He was not concerned about media intrusion. 'I don't think it would worry many soldiers if details of their injuries were made public,' he says. 'It certainly wouldn't have worried me or my family.'

His views are shared by many of the wounded. 'There have been plenty of guys injured – there were guys in Selly Oak next to me who were paralysed from the waist down – but the public are never told of the injuries, and you have to ask why not?'

Jamie Cooper is said to be the youngest British soldier wounded in Iraq. He was blown up by two mortar rounds outside Basra's Shat al Arab Hotel in 2006. But when the 20-year-old was forced to return to civilian life he found little sympathy for his plight.

When he tried to claim council tax disability benefits he was rejected on the grounds that he was not disabled enough.

The first mortar round tore through both of his hands and deeply into the right arm. The second round ripped opened his buttocks and severed the nerves to his leg. From there the shrapnel travelled through his pelvis and into his stomach.

At the time, he found himself evacuated straight from the frontline to an NHS hospital in Birmingham. At Selly Oak Hospital he was forced to spend a night lying in his own faeces after staff allowed his colostomy bag to overflow. Later, the special air mattress used to heal his burns deflated and he was left the entire night in 'considerable pain' despite repeatedly pressing an alarm.

The Observer prompted an enquiry into claims of shocking neglect and appalling treatment of wounded British troops when it published a 'sheaf of complaints' from soldiers' families. The letters were passed on by 'deeply alarmed senior military sources'.

The letters tell of soldiers deprived of adequate pain relief and the problems of being treated within the NHS rather than in dedicated military hospitals. One soldier on a ward with geriatrics, found himself in agony when a confused patient climbed into bed with him.

Another letter complains of having to lie for more than 14 hours in agony because no staff were available to administer pain relief. Shortages of suitable drugs to relive the pain of battlefield injuries are a common theme of the letters.

'The handling of the medical casualties from both Afghanistan and Iraq is a scandal,' insists the former Chief of Defence Staff, Lord Guthrie. He believes the blame does not lie with NHS staff but with senior military medical officers and government ministers who bury their heads in the sand.

Top military and political leaders, he says, 'seem more interested in finding excuses for why things are not good than in correcting them'.

Britain's youngest wounded soldier was offered £57,000 compensation for his multiple injuries which he calls a disgrace, and says the 'lads feel they are being thrown in the gutter'.

'Why is it we need to have a charity 'Help For Heroes' for our facilities even though we should be looked after as a matter of course?' he asks. 'This government needs to do something because it is ruining the country.'

Running on empty

GORDON Brown apparently blew a gasket when he heard the head of the Army demand more for his troops. With the temerity of Oliver Twist, General Sir Richard Dannatt called for urgent change, saying his boys were paid less than traffic wardens and their families were living in appalling housing. And he warned that without action the government would 'break the Army'.

Gordon Brown reacted quickly. He immediately blocked the general's promotion and he issued a statement. He promised that the government would do 'everything in our power . . . to try to reward our armed forces for the dedication and commitment they show'.

The Prime Minister won a few headlines and momentarily upped his ratings but the Army lost a man who many considered the 'cream of the crop'. The former front-line soldier had not been watching his back.

'It was Gordon's decision,' said one Whitehall source. 'Dannatt has made a lot of enemies among the senior reaches of the Labour party.'

Top soldiers who raise their heads above the political parapet are fewer by the day. The SAS is thought to have lost its three most senior commanders after fall-outs with New Labour bosses.

These include Lieutenant Colonel Rick Williams, who resigned after criticism that he paid too much attention to his men's needs, and the most senior SAS commander, Brigadier Ed Butler who opted for more time with his family after being passed over for the post of director of special forces. He was a regular critic of Whitehall.

Politicians must also watch out for crossfire. Conservative Douglas Carswell, MP for Harwich and Clacton, scored a double hit when he criticised equipment failures and apparent cronyism in government contracts on his return from a trip to Afghanistan.

He felt it was his duty to warn that British troops were at risk because of 'inadequate' helicopters but he says the contractors involved tried to silence him. As a key player in the Armed Forces Parliamentary Scheme he suddenly found other members snubbing him. And then he got his marching orders.

'Having learnt from our troops on the ground some of the serious problems with helicopter shortages, and then raised the issue responsibly, I found myself slung off the scheme,' he said. 'Worse, I discovered the scheme is funded by big businesses that might not want too many questions asked about the way the defence budget is currently being misspent.'

Whitehall was keen to play down a report prepared for General Dannatt that painted a shocking picture of life for Britain's soldiers, with reports of under-nourishment, rat-infested homes, and pay so low than many men are officially living in poverty. The report details how thousands of experienced officers and men are leaving the service and how they will never be replaced.

The findings are based on months of interviews with thousands of soldiers and their families between July 2007 and January 2008.

'More and more single income soldiers in the UK are now close to the government's definition of poverty,' says the briefing. 'Thus many married junior soldiers feel that they are being forced to leave because they cannot afford to raise a family on current pay.'

Conditions have deteriorated to the point where 'a number of soldiers were not eating properly because they had run out of money by the end of the month.' And it says commanding officers have been obliged to set up their own 'hungry soldier schemes' where destitute soldiers are loaned money to buy food.

When briefly back from tours of active duty, soldiers are now expected to pay for their own meals in a scheme known as Pay-as-You-Dine, which involves considerable paperwork before men can eat. Previously, the Army provided three square meals a day, all-inclusive, to every serving soldier.

'Now hard-up soldiers have to fill out a form which entitles them to a voucher. The cost is deducted from their future wages, adding to the problems of soldiers on low pay,' explained *The Independent*.

Former colonel and now Conservative MP, Patrick Mercer, says he has spoken to senior officers at length and many believe 'the Army is running on empty'.

'The money has run out,' he says. 'The manpower situation is in crisis and the so-called Military Covenant is abused at every turn. The thing that really worries them is that the MoD seems to be in denial about it.'

MEMBERS' INTERESTS

'We are on the side of ordinary people against privilege, against vested interests of the public or private sector' – Tony Blair.

PERHAPS it resembled a scene from a World War Two film with the departing Germans urgently burning great bundles of papers in a fireplace. While Tony Blair counted down his final days his aides were busy with the shredders. Among the records getting the cross-cut treatment were a number of questionable claims for expenses which the High Court had ordered open to public inspection.

As a lawyer, the New Labour leader must have known that it was a criminal offence to destroy documents if it prevented their disclosure under the Freedom of Information Act. He really should know because he introduced the Act.

It took a lengthy High Court battle before the *Sunday Times* discovered that Mr Blair's Commons staff had shredded the very documents the paper had been trying to obtain for three years.

The paper was finally able to report in early 2008: 'It has now emerged that some of Blair's files covering claims for Myrobella, his constituency home, were destroyed by Commons officials after they rejected the *Sunday Times's* FOI request in January 2005 to see his claims for £43,029 of public money covering a three-year period.'

So keen was Mr Blair to keep the wraps on his expenses and those of others that Commons authorities ran up legal bills of around £500,000 to prevent disclosure.

Good with money

TONY Blair took out a £300,000 mortgage on his constituency home worth half that and claimed back £330.89 a month in expenses from the taxpayer.

The public contributed £10,600 for the Blair's new kitchen, plus £515.75 for the dishwasher. The Prime Minister also claimed £112.26 to have some rubbish removed, and in a five-week period in 2004 put in claims of £933.99 to meet his gas bill.

Although Tony Blair earned just £187,611 as Prime Minister in his final year, he managed to acquire – in additional to Myrobella – a £3.6 million five-bedroom Georgian house in London's elite Connaught Square, two Bristol flats, and a £4 million stately home in Buckinghamshire.

With such financial acumen, he now advises the US investment bank JP Morgan for an annual fee of £2.5 million.

Eye on the cards

IN ADDITION to his duties as Member of Parliament for

Sheffield Brightside David Blunkett managed to find the time to take work advising a US company bidding for Britain's ID card contract. As luck would have it, David knows a thing or two about ID cards.

As Home Secretary, he championed the cause of identity cards and the National Identity Register before having to resign amid accusations that he fast-tracked a visa for his lover's nanny. He went on to promote the controversial cards as Work and Pensions Secretary.

He now advises the Texas-based security company Entrust – which specialises in securing digital information and combating identity theft and is a prime candidate for the identity scheme – and receives up to £30,000 a year.

'David Blunkett was a staunch champion of ID cards and involved right at the heart of the project,' points out former shadow Home Secretary, David Davis. 'The British public will be rightly sceptical about his involvement with a company that could benefit lucratively from this £20 billion scheme.'

Reid's employment

FORMER Defence Secretary John Reid tops up his official salary with an additional £50,000 a year advising a private security company operating in Iraq and Afghanistan.

G4S Security Services now has a highly lucrative contract to train UK forces heading to war zones. It also provides armed security guards to British government employees stationed in war-torn countries.

G4S – thought to be the largest private security contractor in the world – also operates three Immigration Removal Centres in Britain and is responsible for the enforced repatriation of illegal immigrants.

Dr Reid, Home Secretary from 2006-2007, famously said British forces being sent into Helmand would leave again 'without a shot being fired'.

Top earner

TOPPING the list of New Labour MPs making the most of their office is Adam Ingram who served as Armed Forces Minister from 2001-2007.

In additional to his official salary and expenses, he is non-executive chairman of emergency communications company SignPoint Secure Ltd (£45,001-£50,000); and non-executive chairman of design and construction services company Argus Scotland Ltd (£20,001-£25,000).

He picks up an additional £20,001-£25,000 as a consultant to Argus Libya UK LLP; and £50,001-£55,000 as a consultant to Electronic Data Systems Ltd (EDS); plus £10,001-£15,000 from the International School for Security and Explosives Education.

Fruits of Labour

PATRICIA Hewitt, former Secretary of State for both Trade and Health, receives an extra £60,000 a year as a non-executive director of British Telecom. The Leicester West MP was instrumental in the creation of Ofcom, the telecoms and media regulator.

She also holds positions at two private companies: Boots, the high street chemist chain (£45,001-£50,000); and private equity company Cinven (£55,001-£60,000), which has interests in the health sector through its ownership of BUPA's UK hospitals.

Where there's muck

THE minister who helped champion fortnightly bin collections now has a second job with a key player in Britain's multi-million pound waste collection business.

Hilary Armstrong was a local government minister and

served at the Cabinet Office when it paid consultants to advise on bin taxes.

The New Labour member for North West Durham now has a lucrative senior role with the French-owned company SITA which collects rubbish from millions of homes in the UK and wants residents to pay-as-they-throw. They pay her between £30,001 and £35,000 per annum.

Playing by the rules

JACQUI SMITH did absolutely nothing wrong. All she did was declare her main home in the West Midlands to be her secondary home and claim back £24,000 a year from tax-payers while staying at her sister's house in South London.

Ms Smith did nothing wrong because she was following rules written by fellow MPs. She designated a room in her sister's three-bedroom terrace house as her 'main home' and paid a 'market rate' for her lodgings.

She defended the claim, saying: 'As Home Secretary you have to spend the bulk of your time in London. I have always been open. I have played by the rules here.'

Under the rules, the main residence is usually where the MP 'spends more nights than any other'. But people living in the same road as Jacqui's sister Sara describe the Home Secretary's claim as a 'fabrication'.

Jessica Taplin, who lives a few doors down, said: 'She is virtually never here on a Sunday as she claimed and you don't see much of her in the summer. I would say she spends no more than a third of the year here.'

Added value

ELECTED Members of Parliament set their own pay and pensions. According to Ros Altmann of the Pensions Action Group, British MPs 'have voted themselves the most generous pensions of just about anywhere in the world'.

An MP with 20 years' service can expect to receive around £30,000 a year on retirement. The MPs themselves make a contribution of 9.5 percent while taxpayers add a top-up of 38 percent every year.

But Pensions consultant John Ralfe says the true cost to taxpayers could be 48 percent of an MP's £64,000+ salary. They receive an additional £135,850 in expences, including more than £20,000 for living costs.

'Victory for freedom'

PLANS for Honourable Members of Parliament to exempt themselves from the Freedom of Information Act – and thus keep their expenses secret – were abandoned at the last minute by Gordon Brown fearing a public backlash.

The Prime Minister had earlier championed the plan to circumvent a High Court ruling that MPs must provide a receipt-by-receipt breakdown showing how they spend public money on themselves.

A previous attempt to remove Parliament's compliance with the Act was approved by the Commons in 2008 but thrown out by the Lords.

Speaker Michael Martin spent hundreds of thousands of pounds of public money unsuccessfully fighting the High Court case before deciding to change the law in their favour.

Gordon Brown was quick to blame the Tories for dropping out. 'We thought we had agreement on the Freedom of Information Act as part of this wider package,' he said. 'Recently that support that we believed we had from the main opposition party was withdrawn.'

The government had based its argument for exemption from the open government Act by saying MPs had more important things to do than account for their spending.

'It has been argued that it would be excessively burdensome

for Members to have provided receipts for all transactions,' said a committee headed by the Speaker.

Commons Leader Harriet Harman was accused of defying logic when she claimed plans to exempt themselves from the FOI would 'increase transparency' and prove 'a victory for freedom of information'.

MPs' expenses totalled £87 million in 2008.

THE LYNCH MOB REGISTER

'With the increasing sophistication of internal dishonesty, we need to ensure the industry has the most effective tools at its disposal to help reduce losses.' – Mike Schuck, chief executive of Action Against Business Crime.

A GOVERNMENT funded database where workers accused of theft or damage will be blacklisted by employers has been roundly condemned by unions, lawyers and human rights groups. Known as the National Staff Dismissal Register it is being operated as a commercial business.

The register is an 'initiative' of Action Against Business Crime (AABC), which was established as a joint venture between the Home Office and the British Retail Consortium 'to set up and maintain business crime reduction partnerships'.

Major companies including Harrods, Selfridges, HMV, Mothercare and Reed Managed Services have signed up to the scheme. Organisers hope it will also eventually cover the leisure industry, construction and road haulage groups.

Subscribers can check if candidates for jobs have faced allegations of stealing, forgery, fraud, damaging company property or causing a loss to their employers and suppliers.

Workers sacked for these offences will be included on the

register, regardless of whether police have any evidence to convict them. Also on the list will be employees who resigned before they could face disciplinary proceedings at work.

Paul Kenny, general secretary of the GMB, which has 700,000 members, described the NSDR as a lynch mob register that should not be used by reputable employers.

'The fact that the elite who run the companies who run the stores would even contemplate going down this road with the connivance of government shows how far public policy has drifted away from norms of fairness and due process,' he said.

The register has been set up by Surrey-based firm Hicom Business Solutions and will allow employers to search for potential workers by name, address, date of birth, national insurance number and previous employer. Records on individuals – accessible online via an encrypted password system – can include photos.

Mike Schuck, chief executive of AABC, says theft by members of staff costs the British economy billions of pounds each year but rejects any notion that the register is a blacklist.

'We are very pleased indeed to have launched the NSDR and look to it providing an increasingly valuable service to help retailers reduce losses by dishonest staff.'

But workers' groups say this is a clear case of contravention of our justice system. Hannah Reed, TUC policy officer, said: 'The TUC is seriously concerned that this register can only lead to people being shut out from the job market by an employer who falsely accuses them of misconduct or sacks them because they bear them a grudge. Individuals would be treated as criminals, even though the police have never been contacted.'

Mike Schuck is quick to brush aside concerns. All participating companies are obliged to abide by the Data Protection Act, he says, and workers named on the database will have the right to change their entries if they are inaccurate.

But James Welch, the legal director of human rights group Liberty, fears the register does not offer sufficient redress to the falsely accused. 'This scheme appears to bypass existing laws which protect employees by limiting the circumstances when information about possible criminal activity can be shared with potential employers.'

The BBC's website was flooded with comments from people worried by the database. 'This is appalling,' insisted Carol Jay of Grangemouth. 'I know a girl falsely accused of stealing by an employer because she refused his advances. This should be stopped now. Too many innocents could be caught up in it. Only those convicted of dishonesty or assault on co-workers should be included. *Innocent until proven guilty.*'

Paul Kenny of the GMB believes there is every scope for people to be stitched up.

'Getting them on a register like this is tantamount to ensuring that they never work again. Employers faced with employees stealing from them have the same recourse as everybody else – the courts.'

THE DNA SELL-OFF

'Any intrusion on personal privacy is proportionate to the benefits that are gained' – Home Office on the National DNA Database.

THE National DNA Database is being made available to private companies to carry out questionable research on British citizens without their consent. One private company owned by the Home Office has been accused of 'sinister explorations into ethnic profiling'.

'For nearly a decade, the Home Office has been secretly approving controversial research projects using profiles from the DNA database,' says Liberal Democrat MP Jenny Willott. 'No consent was ever sought from the people involved, many of whom have never been charged or convicted of any offence.'

The National DNA Database was established in 1995. Today, around 5.2 million Britons have their unique genetic profile stored on it with new entries added every 45 seconds. The police take DNA samples with or without consent from anyone arrested on suspicion of any recordable offence.

The data can be used to identify a person's relatives and it can tell if someone has Sickle Cell Anaemia or Huntington's disease. Research is underway to use DNA to identify someone's racial origins and their appearance.

When the Liberal Democrats put in a Freedom of Information request in 2008 they discovered that the Home Office had accepted 25 out of 45 requests for DNA samples from various bodies, including commercial enterprises.

Forensic Science Service (FSS), which originally managed the database, is now a wholly-owned private company with all its shares held by the Home Office. It has been carrying out research into the DNA of different racial groups which the Lib Dems see as 'sinister explorations into ethnic profiling'.

The released papers show the FSS received 'samples from each race group to be… used in the race prediction system'. The previously undisclosed Home Office documents show the information will be used to 'create a database for ethnic appearance'.

Other private companies gaining access to the supposedly confidential database include Orchid Cellmark which offers DNA paternity testing services as well as 'immigration testing'; and the Laboratory of the Government Chemists, an 'international leader' offering 'excellence in investigative, diagnostic and measurement science'.

The Human Tissue Act regulates DNA research but exempts the use of DNA for 'purposes related to the prevention or detection of crime'. There are similar exemptions in the Data Protection Act covering consent and the collection and processing of genetic data.

GeneWatch, which monitors developments in genetic technologies, put in a series of FOI requests and discovered a 'lack of transparency about what research is being done and how decisions are made, and failure to keep complete records' and a 'lack of any ethical oversight'.

It also found that the Home Office encouraged 'new commercial products' and that at least one private company maintains its own database of material supplied by the Home Office.

'Unless the government comes clean about exactly what they are using profiles for, this highly dubious ethical practice of dishing DNA out for research must be suspended immediately,' said Ms Willott. 'It's appalling that these big brother practices have been allowed to go on unchecked for so long and with extremely limited ethical standards.'

One group defending commercial participation is the National Police Improvement Agency which operates both in the UK and internationally and offers 'a large and diverse portfolio of products and services designed to support the police service and wider policing family'.

According to a spokesperson: 'They [genetic samples] were made available for authorised research purposes demonstrating clear, potential operational benefit to the police in terms of detecting and solving crime.'

But some say the use of ethnic profiling and 'familial searching' exceeds the bounds of straightforward crime detection.

'The use of people's DNA without their knowledge or consent breaks all ethical and moral standards for research,' insists Phil Booth, national coordinator for No2ID.

'That it was done for profit compounds the offence. And keeping it secret all this time shows that the people in charge knew it was wrong.'

All Wellcome

A GOVERNMENT appointed commissioner has teamed up with private enterprise to produce a report recommending people's medical records and DNA data be made more widely available to pharmaceutical and biotech industries for research.

The report co-authored by Information Commissioner Richard Thomas and Dr Mark Walport of the Wellcome Trust calls for the Secretary of State to approve data-sharing without the need to bother Parliament. And it says 'approved researchers' should be allowed access to data linked to individuals, thus ending any confidentiality.

The Wellcome Trust has campaigned for DNA data to be linked electronically to medical records which critics say would become a backdoor forensic database. The Trust would also like to see a Europe-wide databank.

Research is uncovering which individuals are genetically susceptible to particular diseases. Now there are concerns that people will be specifically targeted to buy expensive medicines and supplements. The commercial potential is enormous.

Additionally, there is no legal bar to human genes being patented by any private companies that discover a link between a gene and a disease, opening the door to another lucrative market.

'People deserve the opportunity to think about what kind of companies they want to have access to this information, and whether controversial practices such as gene patenting should be allowed,' says Dr Helen Wallace, Director of GeneWatch.

Logical steps

THE DNA of every British citizen and visitor to the country should be included in the National DNA Database to 'ensure equality and fairness in the justice system' according to a senior judge who describes the scope of the current database as 'insufficient'.

'It means that everybody, guilty or innocent, should expect

their DNA to be on file for the absolutely rigorously restricted purpose of crime detection and prevention,' says Lord Justice Stephen Sedley. 'I think visitors to this country would have to expect to hand in their DNA too.'

In a BBC interview, he said the government has two choices, either scrap the national database which 'would be ridiculous' or go for one that is 'universal'.

'There is a logic to what Sir Stephen is saying,' admits Home Office Minister Tony McNulty. 'But I think he probably does underestimate the practicalities, logistics, and huge civil liberties and ethics issues around that.'

'How to maintain the security of a database with 4.5 million people on it is one thing,' he said. 'Doing that for 60 million people is another.'

Critics point out that the National Identity Register will contain the fingerprints and iris scans of over 60 million people – which also need to be kept secure.

OPEN SEASON ON BRITS

'The first duty of any government is the protection of its own citizens'
– Geoff Hoon, Minister for Europe [2006-2008].

THE LIVES of British citizens are open to inspection by foreign intelligence agencies on the look out for crimes. The FBI and CIA can now follow the movements of UK drivers in real-time and will soon have access to all our on-line activities and credit card transactions.

Since 9/11, Washington has been gaining access to highly personal information held by both the UK government and by leading British companies. The European Union has also been seeking ways of increasing its share of the intelligence pool.

When the then Home Secretary Jacqui Smith stood before Parliament to read out a list of exemptions to the Data Protection Act she failed to mention that foreign security agencies would now be getting real-time access to the movements of all British motorists.

Two weeks earlier – on the fourth of July 2007 – Ms Smith secretly signed a 'special certificate' giving the CIA and others access to any video feeds from Britain's roadside TV cameras together with the relevant files.

Opponents argue that such open access to our personal data is not helping safeguard our security but simply increasing the chances of it falling into the wrong hands. Others feel uncomfortable that shady intelligence agencies can now trawl through our files on 'data mining' missions.

'This confirms that this government is happy to hand over potentially huge amounts of information on British citizens under the catch-all pretext of national security,' says Nick Clegg of the Liberal Democrats.

Under the agreement, the UK will forward images and data whenever a foreign agency cites terrorism or organised crime as a reason. No evidence is required.

'We would like to reassure the public that robust controls have been put in place to control and safeguard access to, and use of, the information,' says the Home Office.

'It's worrying to see government agencies taking such a cavalier attitude to sensitive data, particularly in the wake of recent scandals in which data on millions of people has been lost by banks and public service contractors,' says Caroline Lucas of the Green Party.

Not wishing to be left out, plans are well advanced in Brussels to form an EU-wide intelligence agency on the lines of the CIA involving all 27 member states. Leading the call for access to our data are France and Germany which head the secretive 'Future Group' that wants to coordinate the work of intelligence services across Europe.

With most agencies reluctant to share information even among their own departments, such a move alarms many inside Britain's secret intelligence community. Although some sensitive information is already exchanged between agencies on a need-to-know basis, openly sharing data is seen as very risky, especially with some European intelligence agencies known to leak like sieves.

The French were accused of handing secret MI6 documents to the Serbs while the Yugoslavia conflict was raging and Israel, a non-member, is continually handed secret EU papers.

'For a long time it has been known that within an hour after being distributed to the member states, all EU documents concerning the Middle East have already reached Tel Aviv, and probably Washington and Moscow,' says the Finnish foreign minister, Erkki Tuomioja.

'There are already well established procedures for sharing sensitive intelligence information to combat terrorism,' says Tory Europe spokesman Mark Francois, who says the Future Group's plans are a step too far.

France and Germany are also keen for the web browsing habits of millions of EU citizens to be scrutinised by the FBI along with their credit card histories. Under a new agreement between Brussels and Washington, previously private data including travel history and spending patterns will be made available.

US terror officials say access to Europe's many databases will help yield valuable information on the movements and habits of potential terrorists.

A few points remain to be ironed out, including provisions for European residents to sue in US courts over mishandling of personal data and whether people's religion, political opinion and 'sexual life' should be included.

'This is outrageous,' insists Sophie in't Veld, a Dutch Liberal MEP on the European Parliament's civil liberties committee. 'This is about fundamental rights. But it has all been done in secret by civil servants behind closed doors.'

They're coming to take you away

A NEW treaty allows the United States to extradite any British citizen without the need for evidence, a tricky provision in the Extradition Act 2003 that has now been removed. The treaty was never debated in Parliament and was only announced to the public and MPs two months after being signed into law.

However, Britain still needs to provide ample evidence if it wants to extradite a US citizen to its shores.

'Under the new treaty, the allegations of the US government will be enough to secure the extradition of people from the UK,' warns Statewatch, which monitors civil liberties in Europe. 'US contempt for the International Criminal Court makes this decision to remove relevant UK safeguards all the more alarming.'

The UK-US extradition treaty, drafted by Home Office officials and their US counterparts, was signed by Home Secretary David Blunkett and US Attorney General John Ashcroft in March 2003.

According to the civil rights group Liberty, the new law is a step in the wrong direction. 'The Extradition Act 2003 undermines longstanding safeguards against unfair removal and unfortunately appears to be more about politics than law,' it insists.

British citizens can now be extradited to over 100 countries – from Albania to Zimbabwe – without the need for evidence.

4
NOT FIT FOR PURPOSE

'The government wants to make this country the best place in the world for children and young people to grow up' – Department for Children, Schools and Families.

SLAMMING the palm of a hand into the base of a child's nose is called a 'nose distraction'. This is just one of various techniques – known as 'restrictive physical interventions'- available to restrain children in custody. When Adam Rickwood was on the receiving end of a 'nose distraction' it produced a lot of blood.

'I asked them why they hit me in the nose and jumped on me,' wrote Adam. 'They said it was because I wouldn't go in my room so I said 'what gives them the right to hit a 14-year-old child in the nose' and they said it was "restraint".'

That night Adam hanged himself with his shoelaces.

The letter was found in his cell at the Hassockfield Secure Training Centre in County Durham, which is run for the Youth Justice Board by Serco Group Plc. The company's motto is 'Bringing service to life'.

Adam was the youngest child to commit suicide in custody. Four months earlier in April 2004 Gareth Myatt, 15, died during another 'restrictive physical intervention' at the Rainsbrook Secure Training Centre in Northamptonshire. Although he pleaded with his three 'custodians' to stop, Gareth was restrained until he choked to death on his own vomit.

'There must be a better way to treat vulnerable children than locking them up like this,' says Deborah Coles, co-director of the pressure group INQUEST. She says 30 children have died in custody since 1990 and describes as an outrage the failure to hold a single public inquiry into conditions in youth detention centres.

Britain – which jails more children than other Western European countries – has been singled out for particular criticism by the United Nations which says thousands of minors are being needlessly criminalised for misdemeanours.

The UN Convention on the Rights of the Child insists children be imprisoned only as a 'very last resort'. Around 25,000 children were given custodial sentences in England and Wales between 2003 and 2006.

A UN report compiled by the four Children's Commissioners for England, Wales, Scotland and Northern Ireland shows that the number of crimes committed by children in the UK has actually gone down over recent years but says convictions have risen by 26 percent.

The number of children under 15 now being criminalised is up by a third and in some parts of the country the overall figure for children being convicted or formally cautioned has almost doubled, according to the Institute for Public Policy Research.

'Current targets to bring more offenders to justice have resulted in the police concentrating on easier-to-solve, low-level crimes committed by children and teenagers who often have complex problems,' says James Crabtree, the institute's associate director of public services.

'This serves to criminalise young people, increases re-offending and misdirects resources from severe offences and crime prevention.'

The Children's Commissioners say the government is in danger of building 'a young criminal underclass'. Where in the past misdemeanours were dealt with by cautions; the trend now is for police to bring charges. And it says new legislation to tackle anti-social behaviour has resulted in more children than ever being drawn into the criminal justice system.

Official figures show that the number of teenagers being jailed is three times that recommended by the criminal justice officials involved in their cases. Over 3,740 offenders aged 18 and under were sent to prison in the 12 months to March 2007, the latest data available. Of these offenders, only around a thousand were recommended for a custodial sentence in their pre-sentence report.

'It is deeply alarming that so many children are being locked up when youth experts do not feel that it is necessary and when we know there is a 92 percent re-offending rate after a young man's first prison sentence,' points out Liberal Democrat shadow home secretary, Chris Huhne.

'These figures blow a jumbo-sized hole in the government's case that custody for children is used as a last resort in this country,' says Andrew Neilson, assistant director of the Howard League for Penal Reform.

'Creative maths'

GOVERNMENT figures purporting to show a dramatic drop in the number of children entering the criminal justice system have been described as a 'smoke and mirrors' exercise because they fail to show that an extra 20,000 received on-the-spot fines.

Rod Morgan, who chaired the Youth Justice Board (YJB) between 2004 and 2007, said the fines handed to youngsters were 'inextricably' excluded from official statistics by 'creative maths'.

According to the YJB, 10.2 percent fewer youngsters were charged with offences between 2005 and 2006 – twice the target of five percent. But Mr Morgan insists the figures exclude juveniles handed out-of-court fixed penalties.

'It does no credit to our criminal justice statistics to perpetrate smoke and mirror exercises of this nature,' he says.

A quiet word

THE Home Office wants police to be able to question children without their parents or other relatives being present. In a 2008 review of the Police and Criminal Evidence Act, ministers called for changes to the rules, dropping the provision that the police must wait for a parent, guardian or other relative. In future, the presence of an 'appropriate adult' – usually a trained lay visitor at the police station – will be sufficient.

Child 'infestation'

BRITONS have a greater fear of their children than anyone else in Europe says the Institute for Public Policy Research. We are more likely to blame young people for anti-social behaviour and are less likely to step in if teenagers cause trouble.

A study by the group found that 39 percent of Britons would avoid a confrontation for fear of physical attack if they saw teenagers damaging a bus stop.

Another poll commissioned by Barnardos found that 49 percent of adults regard children as increasingly dangerous both to each other and to their elders, while 43 percent felt that 'something has to be done' to protect society from children and young people.

More than a third of people agree that 'it feels like the streets are infested with children', over half said children behave like animals and 45 percent agreed that people refer to children as feral 'because they behave this way'.

'Despite the fact that most children are not troublesome, there is still a perception that today's young people are a more unruly, criminal lot than ever before,' says Martin Narey, chief executive of Barnardos. 'The British public overestimates by a factor of four the amount of crime committed by young people.'

'There is a climate of fear,' says Bob Reitemeier, chief executive of the Children's Society. 'The adult population is increasingly afraid of youths and not letting their own children out unsupervised because they are afraid of youth against youth violence.'

The IPPR study found that Britons were three times more likely to cite young people 'hanging around' as a problem than they were to complain about noisy neighbours. It adds that 1.5 million Britons have considered moving to avoid young people hanging around.

'The demonisation of children and young people in some sections of the media and when politicians refer to youngsters as yobs – that breeds the actual fear,' insists Pam Hibbert, principle policy officer for Barnardos.

'The debate about childhood in Britain is polarised between false opposites: that either children or adults are to blame,' points out Nick Pearce, one of the authors of the study. 'In closer knit communities, adults supervise their neighbours' children.

'These days, adults tend to turn a blind eye or cross over on the other side of the road rather than intervene in the discipline of another person's child.'

Bored? Ask Beverley

A GOVERNMENT survey has revealed that most teenagers would like something to do.

The poll of nearly 4,000 teens found 72 percent would prefer to play football, visit the gym or attend a youth club rather than just 'hang about'.

The Teen Talk poll of 16 to 19-year-olds – commissioned by the Department for Children, Schools and Families (DCSF) – discovered that four out of five youngsters think there is not enough for them to do locally.

Topping the list of wished-for activities are football, dance, gym, music and swimming. The poll found that 90 percent felt they were spending 'too much time hanging out at home or with friends' due to lack of opportunities in their area.

The survey forms part of Aiming High for Young People, the DCSF's 10 year strategy to boost 'positive' teen activities.

Demonstrating a clear understanding of the problem, a

DirectGov website is listing local events with suggestions to combat boredom. It recommends that children with nothing to do take up sport or drama and suggests they help save energy and work to stop global warming.

Children's minister Beverley Hughes says it is 'extremely important' to listen to teenagers. 'The Teen Talk survey puts paid to the all too familiar portrayal of them as only being interested in hanging around on the streets or playing computer games,' she says.

Take up a hobby

CHILDREN hoping to take up a hobby are finding that rules designed to keep them safe are barring them from joining model-making clubs or climbing mountains. Adult supervisors are also in short supply fearing accusations of paedophilia and intrusive record checks.

The Safeguarding Vulnerable Groups Act 2006 requires hobby clubs to conduct Criminal Records Bureau checks on all coaches and volunteers or face a fine of £5,000. They must also appoint a child welfare officer and pay for training.

Coaches must give a written explanation of why they want to work with children and provide two references from 'persons of responsibility'.

The Manifesto Club, which campaigns against red tape, found in a survey that most clubs would not now allow children to attend without a parent or approved guardian.

It says: 'Clubs reported that the number of under 18s attending has plummeted from about ten or twenty to one or two, or even none, following their decision to require parents to come too.'

And it says the government has no hope of fulfilling its target to get more teenagers to join sports and hobby clubs unless it changes child protection laws.

'Due to the ridiculous situation now, not only must parents remain with their children but they too must join as a member of our flying club,' says John Bridgett of the Retford Model Flying Club. 'The net result is that junior membership has declined from fifteen down to one over a two-year period.'

Cameron McNeish, editor of *The Great Outdoors* magazine, says it is virtually impossible to find volunteers to take young people mountaineering. 'When I was a kid you joined a club and there was always someone who was willing to take young people out,' he says. 'Clubs don't do that any more as they are scared of the litigation and paedophilia angle.'

The Manifesto Club says there appear to be no winners with modern child protection policies. 'As clubs keep children out, and adults become wary of helping them, young people are deprived of experiences that would help them develop into adults.'

Have a night in

NINE out of ten parents want to see new laws banning their children from leaving the house after dark, according to a YouGov poll for the *Sunday Times*.

'Our poll shows that 73 percent of parents would welcome an 8pm curfew for young children. Similarly, 53 percent would welcome a nationwide 9pm curfew for 10 to 16-year-olds, with a further 35 percent of parents saying a 10pm ban would be acceptable,' reported the paper.

Environment Minister Phil Woolas says: 'There are parts of the country where for periods of time you should be able to introduce curfews. We need a heavy police presence and fines for parents.'

A House of Commons committee has called for a national curfew on young teenagers, saying it would curb anti-social and violent behaviour.

'I have sympathy with the view that children should not be out after 9pm,' adds Keith Vaz, New Labour's chairman of the home affairs select committee.

Residents backed a police-imposed curfew in Redruth,

Cornwall. Children discovered on the streets after dark were 'removed' by police.

Go play with the traffic

GOVERNMENT health advisors are encouraging local councils to turn car parks into sporting and recreational activity centres for children. They hope by using 'non-traditional settings' to raise children's activity levels and cut obesity.

The National Institute for Health and Clinical Excellence wants children to have greater access to parks, woodland and common land to 'stimulate their need to explore'. And it wants to end the assumption that 'the outside is dangerous'. Car parks it suggests could be fitted out with skateboard ramps.

Play away

AN ESTIMATED 2,000 school playing fields have been sold off since New Labour came to power despite a promise to end the practice begun under the Conservatives. Schools Secretary Ed Balls and his predecessor Alan Johnson personally agreed to 19 sales in 2007.

When the Secretary of State for Culture Media and Sport Andy Burnham launched a £36 million 'initiative' for exercise in schools, he praised New Labour's commitment to children's sport, saying 'just 192 playing fields have been sold and all of these were surplus to requirements'.

But official figures reflect less than a tenth of the actual land sold off for development because only the sale of fields over an acre in size need ministerial approval.

'It's not the eighties any more,' insists Andy Burnham, who says school sport is more varied today with kayaking, dodgeball and American football on the curriculum. 'School playing fields aren't being sold off left, right and centre.'

Government spin has seen a pledge to spend £225 million

between 2008 and 2011 on 3,500 new playgrounds and 30 adventure play areas with trained supervisors, plus £100 million for school sport.

In its 1997 election manifesto New Labour promised: 'We will bring the government's policy of forcing schools to sell off playing fields to an end.' Government departments now admit 1,331 'small' playing fields have been sold on to the private sector since 2001.

But pressure group Fields In Trust, which campaigns to save playing fields, insist 'four or five a week' have been sold off since 1997 – more than 2,000 in total.

'We know that they are selling off playing fields,' says Margaret Morrissey of the National Confederation of Parent Teacher Associations. 'What happened to the commitment that they were going to stop the sales? We are doing our children a terrible injustice.'

Children at breaking point
BRITAIN has the unhappiest children in the developed world says UNICEF – the United Nations Children's Fund. The UK came bottom in the survey of 'life satisfaction' among children in 21 developed countries with the poorest and most neglected youngsters.

Britain fails on key measures of poverty and deprivation, happiness, relationships, and bad behaviour, the study showed. The UK came in joint last place with the United States. Northern European countries – The Netherlands, Sweden and Denmark – top the list.

'Young people in the UK are further away than ever from living in a society in which they are valued, respected and enjoyed,' says the Children's Rights Alliance for England, representing more than 100 charities.

In its report to the UN, the Alliance says the government is destroying the childhood of millions by failing to provide sufficient sport and play areas and it says too many exams and the threat of violence has pushed them to breaking point.

The basics of a happy childhood – playing safely outside and enjoying learning at school – are now precious commodities, the report says.

'While ministers – the Prime Minister included – appear comfortable using the language of rights and social justice when talking about children abroad, there is a reluctance to acknowledge that children in England have rights. And that children's rights abuses are happening in our own institutions and communities.'

According to the Institute of Psychiatry, the number of British children with emotional and behavioural problems has doubled in the past 25 years while the number of adolescent suicides has quadrupled.

Critics say the government has totally failed to address the issue with thousands of mentally ill children and teenagers dumped on adult psychiatric wards.

The Children's Commissioner, Sir Al Aynsley-Green, and the charity Young Minds found that only 15 percent of health trusts have complied with the government's commitment that all young people be treated in special units.

It found that mental health services for children are so stretched that 72 percent of inpatient referrals are turned away. It is believed that around 3,000 children and teenagers are placed on adult psychiatric wards each year.

Depressed? Have a Big Mac

POLICE in Sutton are hoping to cut anti-social behaviour by offering discounts on Big Macs, hoodies and computer games. Critics say the 'Positive Citizen' scheme which hopes to 'break down barriers' only encourages sloth and unhealthy eating.

Children between 12 and 17 are eligible for the scheme once they sign a 'good behaviour contract'. They are then given a Positive Citizen photo ID card which allows 10 percent off at

Pizza Hut, New Look and Top Shop. They also receive staff discounts at McDonald's.

'It beggars belief,' claims Neville Rigby of the International Obesity Task Force. 'There's a lot of evidence that eating a diet of junk food makes children behave badly, which means that the police are just creating a problem for themselves in the long-run with these cards.'

Police are confident that the 'initiative' will help win the hearts and minds of the troubled teens of Sutton.

'It will encourage young people to get to know us and give us the opportunity to work together to develop new projects in the future,' explains Sergeant Stuart Taylor-Bard.

Robert Whelan, deputy director of think-tank Civitas, is not convinced. 'If you start thinking you have to pay people who behave, you are admitting the battle has been lost.'

THE ASBO - NOW ANYTHING IS A CRIME

'The government is determined to tackle the scourge of anti-social behaviour which is spreading fear through your community and holding back prosperity' – Home Secretary David Blunkett [2001-2004].

BRITONS' ancient rights enshrined in the Magna Carta were happily brushed aside by David Blunkett when he introduced the Anti-Social Behaviour Order (ASBO) as a key part of the Crime and Disorder Act 1998. Today, a magistrate can classify absolutely anything as an imprisonable offence if it 'causes or is likely to cause harassment, alarm or distress to one or more people'.

ASBOs criminalise non-criminal behaviour. The orders are issued on the lower civil burden of proof (the 'balance of prob-abilities') but incur a criminal penalty if breached. Hearsay evidence is now admissible. ASBOs can be imposed on individuals or groups for a lifetime and in some cases result in people being banished from their own homes. Anyone breaking the terms of an order faces up to five years in prison, the same sentence as possession of a firearm.

Critics say ASBOs are being used to settle old scores between neighbours and that authorities regularly fail to investigate fully before threatening action.

The vagueness of the government's definition of what constitutes 'anti-social behaviour' has seen beggars, prostitutes, drug addicts, the elderly, the mentally ill and children receive the lion's share of the orders.

'When ASBOs were introduced the guidance was that they be used on children only in exceptional circumstances,' insists Martin Narey of Barnardos. 'In some areas the use of ASBOs on children is becoming entirely routine.'

Cathy Evans, from the Children's Society, says: 'We are very concerned at the prospect of creating more ways, more reasons to punish children and to demonise children.'

The British Institute for Brain Injured Children (BIBIC) says over a third of children given ASBOs have underlying brain disorders such as autism and Attention Deficit Hyperactivity Disorder

It cites examples of a 15-year-old boy with Asperger's syndrome who was given an ASBO after a neighbour complained that he regularly stared over the garden fence and another 15-year-old with Tourette's syndrome who was given an ASBO banning them from exhibiting certain symptoms in the street – in this case, the inability to stop shouting obscenities.

'It would appear that the popular phrase 'zero tolerance' was being taken literally,' says BIBIC spokeswoman Pam Knight. 'This is zero tolerance gone potty.'

Jail the sick

A SUICIDAL woman has been banned from going near her

home town's seafront under the terms of an ASBO sought by Aberystwyth police.

Amy Dallamura, 42, has attempted suicide on numerous occasions. In recent years, emergency services have been called out to her at least 36 times.

Aberystwyth magistrates approved the order barring her from entering the sea, the beaches, parts of the promenade and walking on the town's Constitution Hill.

'We took the step of applying for an ASBO because in our view we thought what she was doing was anti-social,' said Inspector Alun Samuel of Dyfed-Powys Police. 'It was causing the public who witnessed what she did distress.'

A woman from Bath who attempted suicide four times received an ASBO that bans her from jumping into rivers, canals or onto railway lines.

Kim Sutton, 23, was rescued three times from the River Avon after trying to take her life. She was also found hanging from a railway parapet. Sutton will now be jailed if she tries to kill herself again.

Magistrates sentenced her for three public order offences after deciding that throwing herself into a river did constitute 'disorder'. The ASBO seeks to prevent her doing anything which could cause alarm or distress to the public.

OAPs on ASBOs

EASTBOURNE'S elderly are receiving more ASBOs than the town's teenagers. Over half the behaviour orders imposed by magistrates at the seaside retirement town are for people over 60.

'When you use the word ASBO, people immediately picture a teenager in a hoodie causing trouble,' says Wendy Megeney, a lawyer with the Crown Prosecution Service in Sussex. 'But the number given to older adults is higher than that given to youths.'

The majority of the town's ASBOs are for 'nuisance behaviour'. These include late-night DIY jobs and touting for gardening work door-to-door.

'I know the town is called God's waiting room but it's no fun being in any sort of room if your next-door neighbour insists on playing her Des O'Connor collection at full blast at 4am,' points out one police officer.

People over 60 account for almost 27,000 of the East Sussex town's population of about 90,000.

Granny in exile

PENSIONER Dorothy Evans has been banned from her own home in Abergavenny, south Wales, for breaching an ASBO. She also received a nine month jail sentence, suspended for two years.

Mrs Evans, 82, was banned from coming within one square mile of the house she has lived in for 41 years after magistrates found her guilty on two counts of harassing her neighbours. She denied 10 breaches of her ASBO which banned her from 'causing harassment, alarm or distress'.

Stop the nuts

A COUPLE who have been feeding squirrels in their back garden for 34 years found themselves facing an ASBO after a neighbour threatened to denounce them to the council.

Fred and Mary Gates of Aylesbury, Buckinghamshire, received an anonymous letter saying they would be reported to the council if the practice continues.

'Grey squirrels are vermin and need to be removed. You are encouraging them by feeding them. If the peanuts do not cease, I will consult my solicitor…and ask the council to seek an ASBO against you.'

In another case, Bernard Hambleton, 66, a life-long pigeon fancier, was given an ASBO by Stockport magistrates after neighbours claimed his feathered friends were putting their lives at risk.

He now faces up to five years in prison if he feed birds near his home or uses 'abusive, insulting, offensive, threatening or intimidating language or behaviour'.

Mr Hambleton, who suffers from throat cancer, has difficulty speaking.

'Pigeons have always been part of his life,' explained his partner, Carole Maiden. 'When he was younger he used to have his own. Now, with the cancer, they are one of his only joys.'

She insists he was targeted as part of a vindictive campaign by neighbours and described accusations of his abusive behaviour as farcical.

'We were shocked when we heard it had gone this far but it only takes a couple of people to get the ball rolling and then it escalates to this.'

Mr Hambleton was also ordered to pay £200 court costs.

Singer silenced

NEXT TIME Caroline Bishop sings in the bath she faces a five-year jail term. A dispute which allegedly began with an autumn bonfire ended when the 39-year-old mother of two found herself slapped with an ASBO.

Neighbours Alistair and Kerry Law called in the council claiming that her sing-a-longs with Bon Jovi and Gary Glitter in a tuneless 'high-pitched noise' were intended to irritate them.

Mr Law told Lincoln Crown Court: 'It was mostly from her bathroom, which is on the ground floor but she would sing outside as well. Sometimes it was three or four times a week.'

Mrs Bishop's legal team claimed the case trivialised the use of anti-social behaviour orders but magistrates disagreed and imposed a two-year order.

In her defence, Mrs Bishop insisted she sang only when she was getting her children ready for school. 'It was just to jolly them along. I don't think I sang loudly. It was just for five or ten minutes.'

She says the dispute has wrecked her life. 'I have nowhere to turn. I have stopped singing. My children live in silence now.'

Piper plugged

PAISLEY schoolboy Andrew Caulfield was ordered to pipe down by Renfrewshire Council for breaking 'anti-social behaviour law noise limits'. If he continues to practise playing the bagpipes in his garden the 13-year-old could be sent to a youth custody centre.

Ironically, the council had asked the teenager to help other youngsters take up the national instrument in a £30,000 campaign to promote pipe playing.

'I've been picked to go round schools to show kids the pipes and play in front of them to promote the council's piping school,' said Andrew, who plays at Paisley Cenotaph every Remembrance Sunday. 'What's the point in teaching kids pipes if they can't practise?'

He was threatened with an ASBO in a written letter from the council after neighbours complained about his music.

'It's very two-faced of the council to be wanting somebody to be involved in the council initiative, yet they're banning him from practising,' said his mother Elaine.

'We've got letters here saying that he could be fined or the instruments confiscated.'

No Pope jokes

POLICE were called in when a man posted a joke about the Pope's death on an alternative village website. He was threatened with an ASBO for 'causing damage' to his local community in the Wiltshire town of Lyneham.

Officers were asked to investigate after Mitch Hawkin posted a spoof advert for the job of pontiff following the death of John Paul II.

His website has been involved in a feud with a similarly named site. The other site's owner, Andy Humm, insists the rival internet presence is bringing 'shame' on Lynham.

Local Conservative councillor Allison Bucknell said: 'An ASBO is being looked at against Mr Hawkin. He's causing a lot of damage to the community.'

ASBO the unborn

BURTON Upon Trent Council threatened to issue an ASBO after receiving anonymous complains that a child was annoying neighbours on his motor scooter. Curiously, Dominic Brown who was accused of the offence had yet to be born.

His mother Julie, 35, who had named her son before he was born, says she is the victim of a cruel hoax and is angry that the council did not bother to fully investigate before it threatened the ASBO.

'It must be the first time an unborn child has been threatened with an ASBO before it's had a chance to do anything bad,' she told the *Daily Mirror*.

Tag for protest Gran

GRANDMOTHER Lindis Percy was lucky to escape an ASBO when the Ministry of Defence and police took her to court for protesting against US military bases in Britain.

Although the judge refused to impose the order, he sentenced the 63-year-old to be electronically tagged and subject to an evening curfew, with £1,000 costs.

The district court hearing in Harrogate was told that Mrs Percy, a part-time health visitor, had committed five offences relating to her regular protests at the nearby US listening base at Menwith Hill.

In rejecting the ASBO order, Judge Anderson said: 'I am firmly of the view courts ought not to allow anti-social behaviour orders to be used as a club to beat down the expression of legitimate comment and the dissemination of views of matters of public concern.'

Her solicitor, Richard Reed, said he believed it was the first time a peace campaigner has been electronically tagged by a court in the UK.

ASBOs passé

GOVERNMENT figures show ASBOs have failed to tackle Britain's 'yob culture'. They also show that around half of all orders are ignored.

However, more than 9,000 people found breaching their ASBOs were imprisoned over a six year period, with an average term of four and a half months.

Then Home Secretary Jacqui Smith, who once described the ASBO as a 'ground breaking innovation', moved on to champion a range of other remedies, such as 'acceptable behaviour contracts'.

'We are not taking it easy on anti-social behaviour – we are getting in early,' she says. 'These early interventions have increased almost fourfold in the past year [2008], putting a stop to problems before they get out of control and before anti-social behaviour orders are required.'

Ms Smith also called for other forms of pressure on alleged criminals, including increased vehicle license checks and more robust investigations into council tax and television licence evasion.

BRITAIN: WHERE FEAR IS OFFICIAL

The Police service in England and Wales will support law abiding

citizens and pursue criminals relentlessly to keep you and your neigh-
bourhoods safe from harm' – The Policing Pledge.

BRITAIN'S police are putting fear into the public but not into the criminals says a report commissioned by the Cabinet Office. The Downing Street document shows people have lost trust in the police and that the criminal justice system rides 'roughshod' over the public.

As such, Britain has become a 'walk on by' society where law-abiding citizens are unwilling to help victims of violent crime because they believe that 'the law is stacked more in favour of offenders than victims'.

The 120-page report compiled by Louise Casey is based on the views of 13,000 people in England and Wales who were consulted over an eight-month period. It says fear of the police 'allows crime to strangle whole neighbourhoods'.

'The public see the criminal justice system as a distant, sealed-off entity, unaccountable and unanswerable to them or to government,' says Ms Casey.

'There was a strong view from members of the public during the review that they would no longer intervene if they saw a crime taking place, for fear that they would either be attacked by the perpetrators or be arrested themselves by the police,' she says.

Then Home Secretary Jacqui Smith admitted the government is aware of the problem.

'Sometimes the criminal justice system can feel remote and appear more interested in supporting offenders than punishing them or protecting communities,' she points out.

To counter the perception, the Policing Pledge was introduced in 2008 to 'increase public confidence that the police and other agencies are dealing with local crime and anti-social behaviour priorities'.

At the core of the new system are the new Neighbourhood Crime and Justice Co-ordinators, local government appointees who act as an active link between the public and the police. They 'aim to impact on perceptions of crime, drugs and anti-social behaviour, mobilise the community to tackle crime, and improve confidence in the criminal justice system'.

The NCJ co-ordinators are part of a £5.6 million 'initiative' to establish a national network of 'neighbourhood crime and justice areas'.

The Policing Pledge promises 'We will always treat you fairly with dignity and respect'.

Spot the victim

ONE MAN who tried to stop a teenager shouting abuse at his wife through the open window of their living room found himself charged with assault. He lost his job as a care worker and now has a criminal record. Magistrates told Stephan Toth that he should never have got involved.

The 34-year-old father of one, who says he is trained to deal with difficult youngsters, tried at first to reason with the boy.

'I went up to him and said, 'Enough is enough'. He said, 'You can't touch me, I'll get you sacked'. I thought his mum should hear this so with open palms I coaxed him towards her house, which is a few doors down.'

When the boy ran off, Mr Toth spoke to the mother and then called the police. They arrived thirty minutes later and took him away.

He says he was surprised to find that he had been charged with assault after the boy's parents claimed he had squeezed the 13-year-old in a bear hug. During the three months it took to bring the case before Margate magistrates, Mr Toth lost his job.

He was eventually told by the chairman of the bench Tony Pomeroy: 'There is insufficient evidence that there was a bear hug causing injuries but the defendant has admitted that he took hold of him by his shoulders and that constitutes an assault in our opinion.'

The chairman criticised Mr Toth for intervening in the first place and advised him to 'just walk away' next time.

Mr Toth feels let down by the criminal justice system. 'I did what any reasonable person would do, yet the law is behind him, not me,' he says.

'I'm the victim here but somehow I've ended up becoming the criminal. Meanwhile, that boy feels like he's above the law.'

No lens on louts

WHEN one householder tried to gather evidence of anti-social behaviour in his neighbourhood by photographing the culprits he was told he was breaking the law and could face prosecution himself.

'We've had problems with this group shouting abuse and throwing stones for months, and were asked to identify them,' David Green, 64, told reporters.

He had earlier appealed to the headteacher of the local comprehensive near London's Waterloo station and was advised to identify the youngsters so action could be taken.

'When I went to take photographs of eight of them throwing cans of coke around, six of them ran away, one threatened to kill me, and another one started phoning the police.'

Mr Green says he was amazed to be accused of assault when a Police Community Support Officer showed up. 'He told me I was not allowed to take photographs of teenagers on the street.'

Mr Green later gave his photographs to the deputy head at the nearby Nautical School and was promised that the matter would be investigated.

'I think it's wrong that when teenagers are running riot and the police are called, it's about me, and I'm treated like a criminal,' said Mr Green.

Police business

A BRISTOL man who photographed a police van ignoring road signs and driving the wrong way down a one-way street to reach a fish and chip shop was arrested and forced to spend five hours in a cell.

Andrew Carter of Bedminster, Bristol, says he was nearly hit by the van. 'So I sort of said, "Hey mate, no entry" but he just shouted out the window, "Fuck off, this is police business".'

'But when I took a photo of them he came running out, battered the camera from my hand on to the floor and arrested me for three crimes, none of which I'd committed.'

Mr Carter was charged with assaulting an officer with his camera, resisting arrest and being drunk and disorderly. The charges were eventually dropped and Mr Carter received an apology.

Sunday night Special

A YOUNG soldier fresh back from Afghanistan has his faith in the police dented along with his head when he was set upon in a case of mistaken identity. Although Wigan magistrates watched video footage of Lance Corporal Mark Aspinall being severely beaten by police they quickly found him guilty of assaulting the officers.

Mr Aspinall, who served seven years in the Royal Electrical and Mechanical Engineers, was sentenced to community service and given a suspended prison sentence. They also ordered that he pay the officers £250 compensation.

The ordeal only ended for the veteran of Iraq and Afghanistan when the CCTV footage was shown again at an appeal court hearing. The judge was so shocked at the appalling police violence that the verdict was over-turned and the officers put under investigation.

Mr Aspinall had been out with friends in Wigan town centre on a Sunday night when he came across three police officers responding to a call that someone was causing a nuisance to paramedics. They quickly assumed the 24-year-old was to blame.

The footage shows the officers moving in on the stationary soldier. He is then rugby tackled to the ground and the beating begins. Special Constable Peter Lightfoot, an unpaid and part-time officer weighing in excess of 20 stone, is seen repeatedly punching the defenceless man on the base of his neck. The assault only stopped when a passing motorist slowed down to watch.

'I was scared for my life,' said Mr Aspinall. 'I remember thinking, I'm going to die here. I can't believe I've survived Afghanistan and Iraq and now I'm going to die on this main road in my home town at the hands of the police. Yet I was the one who ended up in the dock, not the officers.'

He was then bundled into a police van in handcuffs, with injuries to his face and neck, and taken to Wigan police station where he was held in custody for 20 hours. He was then charged with two counts of police assault and a public order offence.

'It was awful. I had come back from fighting in Afghanistan and now, on community service, I was painting a school as a convict, standing next to men who were drug dealers and robbers,' said Mr Aspinall.

When his appeal came through four months later, Judge Phipps at Liverpool Crown Court expressed deep concern, both at the police and the criminal justice system.

'Where is this man of violence?' he asked. 'I am shocked and appalled at the level of police violence shown here.' He went on to express 'great concerns' about the police action shown on the CCTV footage and he questioned the truthfulness of the officers' statements.'

'I would go as far as to say the statements contain untruths,' he added.

Gardener in scythe drama

IT TOOK Peter Drew eight months to clear his name after police found offensive weapons in his car and began dragging him through the courts. The 49-year-old gardener had been found in possession of axes, a machete and a scythe.

Although he was quick to produce references proving his occupation, the Crown Prosecution Service forced Mr Drew, of Heamoor near Penzance, Cornwall, to suffer months of court appearances. It eventually dropped the charge minutes before the trial.

He described the ordeal as a nightmare. 'The whole thing knocked me for six. I've lived in Heamoor all my life and when the case was reported in the papers, people were asking me what it was all about and I didn't want to say anything because the case was still going on.'

The judge eventually ordered the CPS and police to apologise but Mr Drew believes the false charge damaged both his business and reputation.

'I'm disgusted, really. Now I just want to clear my name so everyone knows I haven't been carrying knives illegally.'

Knife twist

FAST food stall holder Jane Bellas was arrested by police when they discovered a kitchen knife in her car. Although she explained to officers that she used it to slice bread rolls she was charged with having a knife in a public place without good reason.

But when she appeared at Carlisle Crown Court to face up to four years' imprisonment the judge dismissed the charge after evidence was presented showing that she had a valid reason to possess a knife, namely her occupation.

'There's a lack of common sense in the way that laws are being enforced,' says solicitor John Smith. 'If they had looked into this in more detail at an earlier stage it might have been resolved sooner.'

Miss Bellas, 29, was formally found not guilty and given £10 to cover travelling expenses. Her DNA and fingerprints remain on file.

Police take stick

KENT police were on alert when they spotted a 78-year-old man using a walking stick. They quickly surrounded the retired classics teacher and told him the 3ft cane was an offensive weapon.

The officers, who had been monitoring climate change protesters, confiscated Philip Clarkson Webb's walking stick and gave him a receipt. 'But later when I produced my receipt and asked for the stick it was curtly refused,' he said.

He later received an apology from Kent Police but not the walking stick.

'I don't believe it!'

THERE was no apology for 82-year-old Frank Gibson, a former mayor of Gravesend, governor of two schools, trustee on two charities, holder of an OBE, and arthritis sufferer who walks with a stick.

He was taken aback when two police officers pulled him over in his car on Christmas Eve 2006 on his return from midnight mass. He was even more amazed to find the officers struggling to restrain him. They radioed quickly for back-up, cuffed his hands and bundled him into the back of a squad car.

'At one point, there were five officers at the scene – and seven at the police station – to keep this old man in check,' he says. 'It's a fairy story, isn't it? I don't have the wit to invent a story like this.'

He was held overnight in police cells and only released at dawn. 'I was very depressed all Christmas Day,' he says. 'It wrecked Christmas.'

According to the two young officers, the pensioner assaulted them both, pushing one in the chest and twisting the thumb of the other. But Mr Gibson told Medway Magistrates' Court that he was too weak to assault anyone.

However, the court rejected his version of events. The chairman of the bench, Mrs Angela Howe, said Mr Gibson had 'allowed his temper to get the better of him'. She found him guilty and ordered that he pay costs of £910. He was also given a six-month conditional discharge.

On hearing the verdict, Mr Gibson is reported to have slumped forward and whispered, 'I can't believe it.'

Safety first

WEST Yorkshire police shot Nicholas Gaubert twice with electronic stun guns after he collapsed into a diabetic coma on a bus. Officers fired the 50,000 volt Taser weapons into him because he 'refused' to obey instructions.

The two officers, who had been issued with Tasers just two weeks earlier, were called to the empty bus when the driver reported a man slumped in his seat at the end of the route in Headingley.

'I think the officers involved just saw it as an opportunity to try out their new toys,' explained Mr Gaubert, 34, a bistro owner and son of a magistrate. 'It should have been obvious that I was having a 'hypo' and I wear a necklace alerting people I am diabetic.'

Police later told him that he had to be blasted twice because he fell from his seat after the first shock and lay face down with one hand beneath his body. The officers felt it was unsafe to approach so shot him again. He was then taken unconscious in handcuffs to the police station.

The Crown Prosecution Service said no charges would be placed against the two policemen after an investigation concluded they had not breached health and safety guidelines.

'I am absolutely disgusted that no action will be taken,' said Mr Gaubert. 'I was totally innocent. The only thing that could have made people suspicious was that I had a black rucksack with me. If I was planning to blow up the bus, why didn't I do it when there were passengers on board?'

He says he still has nightmares about the attack and describes what happened as a 'chilling precursor' to the shooting of Jean Charles de Menezes in London one week later.

'What goes through my mind now is what would have happened if they had been carrying real guns like they were in London. It gives me nightmares.'

The Home Office wants even more Tasers in the hands of the police and is spending £8 million to train all 30,000 front-line officers in their use.

'Everyday the police put themselves in danger to protect us, the public. They deserve our support, so I want to give the police the tools they tell me they need to confront dangerous people,' then Home Secretary Jacqui Smith explained.

'That is why I am giving the police 10,000 Tasers to ensure that officers across the country benefit from this form of defence.'

Taser weapons work by enducing electro-muscular disruption that causes the nerves and muscles to contract violently. The latest version – the X26 – implants copper barbs into the skin or clothing from up to 26 feet.

The weapons have been described by Amnesty International as 'potentially lethal'.

'They can inflict severe pain at the push of a button, without leaving substantial marks,' says the group's arms programme director Oliver Sprague. 'The Taser is clearly a dangerous weapon and should only be used in very limited circumstances where strictly necessary to protect life or avoid very serious injuries.'

Around 290 people have died in the US and Canada after being shot with the stun guns since 2001. In 90 percent of cases, the victims were unarmed. Many were shot repeatedly.

Llandudno police cited 'safety reasons' for zapping an 89-year-old man with the weapon when he was found wandering the streets in a confused state. He had earlier run away from a residential care home where he was said to be unhappy.

The man, a retired carpenter and war veteran who asked not to be named, is the oldest person in Britain to be targeted by the new weapon. Police said he was holding a shard of broken glass and threatened to kill himself when officers tried to take him back.

'In the circumstances, the specially trained officers made the judgment, in order to protect the life of the man, that the use of Taser was the safest and most appropriate option,' said a police spokesperson.

North Wales Police said it would not be referring the incident to the Independent Police Complaints Commission.

'The police say he was holding a shard of glass to his neck but we think they should have tried persuasion,' said his nephew. 'It's a miracle he didn't have a heart attack on the spot.'

'We've been told his arms were handcuffed behind his back, which we don't think is the way to treat an old man who had never been in trouble in his life. He says the pain was excruciating and that he was frightened to death.'

HOW OFFENSIVE ARE PUPPIES?

'The whole point [of] multicultural Britain was to allow people to live harmoniously together, despite their difference; not to make their difference an encouragement to discord' – Tony Blair.

THE government's policies aimed at creating a cohesive multicultural Britain are dividing more people than they unite. Critics say over-sensitivity to one religious group is forcing the rest of the population to tread on eggshells. It alienates one group and annoys almost everybody else. Many argue that the government would do better by treating all sectors of the community equally because attempts at avoiding offence are doing just that, and predictably so.

When Tayside police dropped a clanger with their new advertisement featuring the loveable Alsatian puppy Rebel they quickly tried to make amends. But far from helping heal a divided community they simply widened the rifts.

'We did not seek advice from the force's diversity adviser prior to publishing and distributing the postcards. That was an oversight and we apologise for any offence caused,' explained a remorseful spokesperson for the force.

Rebel the six-week old puppy – who had been given his endearing name by children at St Ninian's Primary School in Dundee – had put his paw right in it. He had unthinkingly offended Muslims.

'The advert has upset Muslims because dogs are considered ritually unclean,' explained the *Daily Mail*. The story prompting reader Declan to comment 'Here we go again'.

'Some people really need to get to grips that if they want to live in this country then they have got to get used to our ways not the other way around. Outrage over a little dog – what next?'

The source of the 'Muslim outrage' was reported to be local councillor Mohammed Asif who had 'raised the issue' with the chief constable. The British National Party swiftly updated its website and offered supporters a pre-packaged appeal to Tayside police.

'I find the comments attributed to Dundee councillor, Mohammed Asif, by *The Mail* to be racially offensive and extremely divisive and, in my view, worthy of investigation by the Tayside Hate Crimes Unit. Would you therefore please confirm that Tayside Police will launch an investigation into the alleged remarks by Mr Asif, as I feel deeply hurt by what he said.'

When *The Telegraph* ran the story it also gave dozens of readers an opportunity to vent their feelings. The time to dance on eggshells was over. Rebel the puppy had done just what Mr Blair had tried to avoid. This was all-out 'encouragement to discord'.

'I've never heard so much grovelling tripe,' wrote reader 'Sebastian'. 'Utterly pathetic. They're yielding to medieval superstition and idiocy which we can do without in Britain. Impure? Unclean? Ritual washing 7 times? Complete bullshit. Why do we – any of us – put up with this?'

Digs against Britain's 'soft' new persona came from across the Atlantic. One American reader was perplexed. 'Are you the same Britain that led allied forces in WWII, the same Britain that stood against Nazism, totalitarianism, ruthless dictators; the same Britain that produced Churchill, CS Lewis, William Wilberforce, heck even, Winnie the Pooh?' asked Dana.

A number of Muslim readers were equally perplexed by the story. 'I don't think anyone should find it offensive, nor should there be an apology. As for finding dogs ritually unclean...the person who said that is a flipping idiot,' wrote Khan. 'Would you Brits STOP capitulating to Islamists!'

Pig-free banks

PERHAPS Nat West believed they had so few Muslim customers because of an unintended slight. They must have scratched their heads and wondered where they were going wrong. And then the penny dropped. Overnight, all piggy banks and their effigies were banished and the high street bank would hence forth be pork-free.

Despite the sacrifice, it seems few if any Muslims opened new accounts perhaps because their religion opposes the lending of money with interest. The move did, however, draw the inevitable story in the *Daily Star*.

'Muslims do not eat pork, as Islamic culture deems the pig to be an impure animal,' explained the paper. It had earlier called the Lancashire Council of Mosques and asked for a quote.

The secretary, Salim Mulla, obliged. 'This is a sensitive issue and I think the banks are simply being courteous to their customers,' he diplomatically explained. It was easier to find 'accusations of political correctness gone mad'.

'The next thing we will be banning Christmas trees and cribs and the logical result of that process is a bland uniformity,' the Dean of Blackburn, Reverend Christopher Armstrong, said indignantly.

Pigs in cupboards

SCHOOLS with high numbers of Muslim pupils are removing all references to pork and pigs generally. Under-sevens in Batley will no longer have to hear stories about unclean animals.

'Recently I have been aware of an occasion where young Muslim children in class were read stories about pigs,' explained a horrified head teacher. She promptly banned books with pigs from the classroom to avoid offence.

'We try to be sensitive to the fact that for Muslims talk of pigs is offensive,' explained Barbara Harris. 'The books remain in the school library and there is nothing to stop our younger children having stories such as "The Three Little Pigs" in small groups.'

Where's Piggy?

A BOOK featuring no pigs whatsoever has been banned in case Muslim readers confuse 'The Three Little Cowboy Builders' with another work that does have pigs in it.

The book's publishers say it was rejected for an award after judges became concerned that it would offend Muslims. The animated virtual book for primary school children was also criticised for its potential to offend builders.

Ann Curtis, whose company Shoo Fly Publishing produced the CD-Rom, said the judges on the Bett Awards – supported by the government's schools technology agency Becta – might even 'propagate a racist stance' themselves.

'I felt disbelief, to be honest,' she explained. 'As a small company we have a strong ethical and moral grounding. We support the rights of all children in the world to have access to education.'

'To be told that we cynically set out to alienate minority groups is a very narrow-minded view.'

Sensitive skin

THE Home Office refused to issue a baby with a passport claiming his topless picture could upset Muslims. *The Sun* says mum Tracey Barnes was 'furious' when bureaucrats returned photos of bare-chested son Lewis.

'It's so politically correct it's untrue,' insisted Tracy. 'Lewis wasn't born with a stripy top on.'

Photos sent to the Passport Service were returned marked 'not acceptable for passport purposes as the child appears to be unclothed'. Helpline staff explained that the exposed skin might be considered offensive in a Muslim country.

Another youngster whose shoulders were deemed too sensitive for the Muslim world had her application rejected at the Post Office. Her parents were told other applications had been turned down for the same reasons.

'This is quite ridiculous,' said the girl's mother, Jane Edwards. 'I followed the instructions on the passport form to the letter and it was still rejected. How can the shoulders of a five-year-old girl offend anyone?'

A spokesperson for the Identity and Passport Service said it was not its policy to reject applications with bare shoulders but suggested Post Office counter staff might be 'sensitive to these things'.

Crossed off

HOT CROSS buns have been wiped off the menus of schools across Britain following a government edict that local authorities must abandon the ancient Easter tradition to avoid upsetting children of non-Christian faiths.

The London borough of Tower Hamlets had earlier made a unilateral decision to remove the buns from menus after coming under fire for serving pancakes on Shrove Tuesday. A spokesperson for the New Labour-run council claimed that there had been 'a lot' of complaints but could not give a figure.

'We are moving away from a religious theme for Easter and will not be doing hot cross buns. We can't risk a similar outcry over Easter like the kind we had on Pancake Day. We will probably be serving naan breads instead.'

The Muslim Council of Britain was quick to label the decision as 'very, very bizarre'. A spokesman said: 'This is absolutely amazing. British Muslims are hardly going to be taken aback by a hot cross bun.'

'Unfortunately actions like this can only create a backlash and it is not very thoughtful. I wish they would leave us alone. We are quite capable of articulating our own concerns and if we find something offensive, we will say so. We do not need to rely on other people to do it for us.'

Nil by mouth

THE TEA trolley at Tower Hamlets Council in East London had to be laid up for the duration of Ramadan – the Islamic month of fasting – following a proclamation from above. In an email from the head of 'democratic services', all elected members were advised to follow strict Islamic fasting no matter what their faith.

The council – which in the past turned Christmas lunch into a 'festive meal' and burnt a Bengal tiger on Bonfire Night – was presumably hoping that the people's representatives might use the opportunity to better themselves.

During the Holy month, participants seek forgiveness for past sins, pray for guidance and help in refraining from everyday evils, and try to purify themselves through self-restraint and good deeds. They must also forgo all food, drink, chewing-gum, tobacco, and sex until the sun sets.

Dr Stephanie Eaton, leader of the Liberal Democrat group, said she did not want to abstain and found the whole thing 'disconcerting'.

'We fervently believe that the rules of any one religion should not be imposed upon others. This sends out the wrong message to our community,' she told a reporter for the *Daily Mail*.

'Our community consists of a huge number of different religions, all of which should be valued, and no one religion should be accorded more status or influence than others.'

Let there be light

SCHOOLS that ban Christmas for fear of giving offence are making matters worse by failing to realise that Jesus is also an Islamic prophet. Such ignorance say scholars sets a poor example to students and upsets parents of both faiths. And it also stirs up the bigots.

When the predominantly Asian Walter Street Primary School in Burnley decided to drop the 'Virgin' from Mary's accepted title, they quickly received some religious instruction.

'The Virgin Mary is covered extensively in a chapter of the Koran and Muslims believe Jesus, praise be upon him, was born from an immaculate conception,' explains Anjum Anwar, chairman of the Lancashire Forum of Faiths. 'The Virgin Mary is also considered a role model. Muslims don't want to see Christmas diluted.'

Headteacher Sarah Watson explained that the school – which was singled out for praise by the government watchdog Ofsted – needed to 'tread a line between two faiths'.

She said 'appropriate versions' to chart Christ's birth were needed as 90 percent of the 370 children at the school are of Pakistani descent.

Ofsted's often confusing edicts were blamed when the Yorkshire Coast College re-branded Christmas and Easter in its annual calendar. The local Tory MP was quick to climb his high horse.

'This is absolutely barmy,' Robert Goodwill told reporters. 'We are a Christian country and, to be honest, religious tolerance in this country is about respecting other people's religious beliefs.

'They are petrified that they offend the minority but what they are doing is offending the majority,' he says. 'I am disappointed that it's from an edict from Ofsted.'

The Scarborough-based college, which specialises in teaching 'life skills', said it was only following orders and that it had used Ofsted guidelines to 'increase inclusion and diversity'.

With ignorance seemingly emanating from the top, religious leaders blame politicians and town halls for fuelling right-wing extremism. The Christian Muslim Forum says they are playing into the hands of extremists who blame Muslim communities for undermining Britain's Christian culture.

BNP leader Nick Griffin sees the potential in Britain's Muslim population as a sure-fire vote-winner.

'We bang on about Islam. Why?' he asks. 'Because to the ordinary public out there it's the thing they can understand. It's the thing the newspaper editors sell newspapers with.'

The Forum says government attempts to forge a multi-faith society, together with attempts at avoiding offence, are sparking growing anger among Christians and other faiths.

'They provoke antagonism towards Muslims and others by foisting on them an anti-Christian agenda they do not hold,' it says, adding that it can only 'backfire badly' on the Muslim community.

'Sadly, it is they who get the blame – and for something they are not saying.'

CCTV – WHY ALL THE CAMERAS?

The extent of CCTV coverage and the government's funding of new systems has increased dramatically over the last decade. There is very little substantive research evidence, however, to suggest that CCTV works' – NACRO Crime and Policy Section.

BRITAIN'S CCTV cameras are next to useless when it comes to preventing or solving crime say some of the country's top policemen. Despite billions of pounds of public money very few people are ever convicted while the majority of the cameras are illegal under the government's own rules.

The UK is regularly cited as the most observed society in the Western world with one-fifth of all CCTV cameras on earth. Politicians argue that the public want street cameras because it not only makes them feel safer but acts as a deterrent for criminals.

But with so many images produced every second, effective monitoring is difficult and many police admit they despise having to trawl through hours of footage. A Home Office report found that 80 percent of images given to police are worthless as evidence. CCTV footage as court evidence is extremely rare.

The London bombings in July 2005 were described by the Metropolitan Police as the largest criminal inquiry in English history but no moving CCTV footage of the bombers on the day has ever been shown to the public.

Although the majority of London buses are fitted with sur-veillance cameras, no images were available from inside the number 30 bus in Tavistock Square. The congestion charges cameras also failed to spot the bus. And, although one unedited still has been produced of the four at Luton station, no moving CCTV footage is available of the group on their travels on Thameslink Rail or the London Underground system on the day of the bombing.

In all, only three percent of crime in London is ever solved using CCTV footage. Many question the need for cameras at all.

The value of privacy

HAMPSHIRE'S deputy chief constable is so worried about public surveillance that he says he no longer wants to live in a country that has cameras on every street corner. When Ian Readhead's own sleepy little town of Stockbridge had CCTV installed he found himself asking why.

'Does the camera actually instil in individuals a great feeling of safety?' he asked. 'Does it prevent serious offences taking place?'

After his local parish councillors spent £10,000 installing CCTV, crime actually went up with a total of two violent crimes reported between 2005 and 2006.

'I'm struggling with seeing the deployment of cameras in our local village as being a benefit to policing,' the police chief told the BBC. 'If it's in our villages – are we really moving towards an Orwellian situation with cameras on every street corner? I really don't think that's the kind of country that I want to live in.'

The Police Federation has its concerns. Vice chairman Alan Gordon says: 'I have sympathy with members of the public who are not going to be committing crimes and feel they are being spied on. It should be down to consultation with people locally,' he says.

Stockbridge parish council chairman David Baseley defended the need for public surveillance. 'We were concerned about the vulnerability of the place, although we haven't had any real crimes,' he admits.

'Politicians like to present the police as ever hungry for more powers,' points out Shami Chakrabarti of Liberty. 'Yet even the police are concerned that we are losing the value of privacy.'

A better image

CCTV is only failing because not enough people are being convicted says the senior police officer charged with setting up a new nation-wide surveillance image database. He wants to see more money spent on advanced technologies and he wants the people operating the cameras to feel valued.

'It's been an utter fiasco: only three percent of crimes were solved by CCTV,' says Detective Chief Inspector Mick Neville, who heads Scotland Yard's Visual Images Identifications and Detections Office (Viido).

'Billions of pounds has been spent on kit but no thought has gone into how the police are going to use the images and how they will be used in court,' he claims.

To help boost confidence and convictions, Viido is currently setting up a nation-wide image database using technology developed by the sports and advertising industries that allows cameras to track a person's movements across a city by concentrating on the logos on their clothes.

Images of suspects as well as convicted criminals will be added to the database. Biometric companies are collaborating on technology that actively seeks out known or suspected offenders from CCTV footage using 'facial mapping techniques' and matches it to the databases.

Inspector Neville says they have already begun collating images from across London. 'We are also going to start putting out [pictures] on the internet, on the Met police website, asking "who is this guy?"'

Concerns that innocent people will find their images on a virtual ID parade have been dismissed. Information commissioner Richard Thomas believes there are sufficient safeguards in the system to nip any abuse in the bud.

'We would expect adequate safeguards to be put in place to ensure the images are used only for crime detection purposes, stored securely and that access to images is restricted to authorised individuals,' he says.

But one watchdog believes the commissioner is not working hard enough. Gordon Ferrie of CameraWatch says the vast majority of surveillance cameras may be breaching the Information Commissioner's own code of practice as well as the Data Protection Act.

'Our research shows that up to 90 percent of CCTV installations fail to comply with the Information Commissioner's code of practice and that many installations are operated illegally,' he insists.

Under the code of practice and the Data Protection Act, CCTV cameras must be visible with clear signs. Camera operators also have an obligation to prevent images being shared with outside parties.

The findings have 'profound implications for the reputation of the CCTV and camera surveillance industry and all concerned with it,' he says.

Inspector Neville believes that while further investment in new technology is essential, more work must be done to boost the image of the surveillance industry as a whole and to make its operatives feel valued. Currently, many police officers are put off he says 'because it's hard work'.

'CCTV operators need feedback. If you call them back, they feel valued and are more helpful,' he says, adding that he wants to expand the surveillance side of policing. 'We want to develop a career path for CCTV inquirers,' he says.

DNA - SO WHO'S STUPID?

'So I know for example with the DNA database that tens of thousands of crimes have been solved because of the use of the DNA database' – Home Secretary Jacqui Smith (2007-2009).

FIGURES on the number of crimes solved using the National DNA Database are extremely hard to come by. This has not stopped ministers from trumpeting the success of a system which many consider both seriously flawed and the ultimate intrusion into our lives.

Britain leads the world in storing the genetic profiles of its citizens. Police in England and Wales can take DNA samples without consent from anyone arrested on suspicion of any recordable offence. This can range from begging and drink offences to partaking in an 'illegal' demonstration.

The information is stored as DNA profiles – the string of numbers used for identification purposes – and DNA samples which contain a person's entire genetic make-up. These are kept permanently even if the person is released without charge or later acquitted by a court. Under Scottish law, police cannot store the DNA samples of innocent people.

Gordon Brown insists thousands of people have been successfully prosecuted using DNA evidence. 'I say to those who questioned the changes in the Criminal Justice and Police Act 2001 which allowed DNA to be retained from all charged suspects even if not found guilty: if we had not made this change, 8,000 suspects who have been matched with crime scenes since 2001 would in all probability have got away, their DNA having been deleted from the database.'

The Prime Minister's figures – which may have come as a surprise to the court service – had not previously been made public, despite repeated calls from opposition parties. He insisted: 'This includes 114 murders, 55 attempted murders, 116 rapes, 68 other sexual offences, 119 aggravated burglaries and 127 drugs offences.'

The claims were met with broad derision. 'Gordon Brown has stooped to a new low to claim that 114 murderers 'would in all probability have got away' if innocent people's DNA records were deleted,' said Dr Helen Wallace, Director of GeneWatch UK.

'This claim is both ridiculous and entirely false. DNA *matches* are not *solved* crimes – many matches occur with victims and with passers-by, or are false matches.'

GeneWatch says numerous MPs have requested figures on the number of crimes solved by retaining DNA profiles from innocent people. 'In each case, ministers have replied that this information is not available,' it says.

DNA has uses beyond crime detection. Access to the genetic data of Britain's population would be valuable to foreign intelligence agencies, insurance companies and bio-tech industries. Even criminals tracking down the family of a witness would find DNA linked to an address to be useful. Many question if the government and the private sector will be able to keep the data secure.

'We fear that they will allow hackers to penetrate the system and grab our genetic details, that future governments may use the information it contains about our health or families to bully and bribe us, that cash-strapped ministers may sell our details to commercial organisations,' explains Edward Heathcoat-Amory, the *Daily Mail's* leading political columnist.

'If we trusted our leaders without reservation, we would have far fewer concerns about allowing them to store our DNA details,' he says.

Security Minister Lord West believes the National Database must be made available to foreign intelligence agencies in the fight on terror. 'There is a real need to share this data internationally, especially where terrorism is concerned,' he says.

'During surveillance, a DNA sample may be obtained without a warrant. A good example might be where a person discards a cigarette or a drinks container. It can be collected covertly and a sample taken,' he explains.

He says covert human intelligence agents 'could visit the source's house and a sample could be taken from a teacup.' The sample is then added to the National DNA Database.

'We can now obtain profiles from something that may have been only touched, and match DNA from just a few cells,' says Professor Allan Jamieson, director of the Glasgow-based Forensic Institute.

'From a system that had match probabilities of thousands, we are in the era of billions. This is where the problems begin. For many cases, the issue is not: "Is it my DNA?" It is: "How did it get there?"'

The simple discovery of DNA at a crime scene automatically sets the police on a path of investigation that may be no more than circumstantial, he says. And it can easily lead to wrongful convictions.

'The police are likely to conclude on the basis of a database match that they are investigating the guilty party. The investigative process can then follow a pattern of accumulating circumstantial evidence. Once this process results in a charge, an error can be compounded by the jury failing to appreciate the difference between threads of evidence all dependent on that first 'identification' by DNA.'

When the European Court of Human Rights ruled in late 2008 that keeping DNA samples of innocent people breaches their human rights, the Home Office wrote to police forces around the country telling them to ignore the ruling.

Although Jacqui Smith announced that DNA samples of children under 10 would be removed immediately – an estimated 70 samples – she announced plans to allow police to trawl the country taking samples from serious offenders who have been released from jail.

Increasing the size of the DNA database will not make it any easier to find criminals says GeneWatch. 'The chances of detecting a crime using DNA have not increased over the last five years, despite a doubling in size of the DNA database.'

Dr Wallace points out: 'People are not stupid – they know that keeping their children's DNA when they've done nothing wrong is not helping to solve crimes.'

GORDON'S CARD TRICKS

'It is important to recognise we cannot promise that every single item of information will always be safe because mistakes are made by human beings. Mistakes are made in the transportation, if you like

in the communication, of information' – Gordon Brown.

ALMOST half the British public think compulsory biometric ID cards are a good idea because they will thwart terrorists, exclude illegal immigrants and reduce fraud. They will allow us to prove our identity whenever our papers are demanded and they give the State immediate access to our life history. The rest of the population are either unconcerned or think ID cards are a very bad idea.

At the heart of the system is the National Identity Register. The cards are just the visible manifestation of the huge database beneath. All existing databases will eventually be linked to the NIR along with the new e-passports that keep track of our international movements. This information is passed on automatically under the e-Borders scheme to 'contributing countries' that share travel data.

By entering a person's NIR number into a terminal, access will be gained to a person's school record via the mammoth Contact Point child database, to medical records, criminal records, arrests sheets, political affiliations, benefit entitlements and contact with social services, plus DNA profile with ethnicity.

Additional links to the databases of biotech industries and other multinationals will give access to employment records, credit history, and levels of alcohol consumption.

The Identity and Passport Service says 265 government departments and around 44,000 private sector organisations will be 'accredited' to verify peoples' identity using the register.

'Each time anyone checks on your ID, it will be recorded. That means that over time the authorities could build up a very accurate picture of everything you do,' says Phil Booth of No2ID.

'That audit trail then becomes the key to the data that is stored on all other databases, no matter where they are kept. It is not necessary to have a giant database because your ID number and the audit trail provide the key to the information on all the other databases.'

Under government plans, ID cards will be held by everyone over 16 from 2017. From 2010, people under 18 can volunteer for a card.

'It's not just the sheer amount of personal information that you will be required to surrender, it's the threats that will be used to force compliance,' explains No2ID, which campaigns against threats to privacy and liberty.

'You could have £1,000 penalties sent to you by e-mail,' they point out. 'If you fail to turn up at a time and place of their choosing; refuse to be fingerprinted, photographed or hand over documents; fail to tell them you've moved house for three months – and anything that they reckon is 'deliberate or reckless' provision of incorrect information could lead to two years in prison.'

The Home Office can enter information in the National Identity Register without informing the individual. All entries are presumed to be accurate, although there is no duty to ensure that the data is accurate.

The government's own figures show that just one government department has a system in place to correct data errors. A Freedom of Information request by identity management company Garlik revealed that just one department has a procedure in place to correct errors within its databases – the education watchdog Ofsted.

'When you see it written down in department after department, 'no we haven't been audited, no we don't have any written policies, no we don't have a budget, no there are no statistical information,' it does take you aback,' said Garlik's chief executive, Tom Ilube,

'What it says to me is that these departments are not taking looking after personal information seriously. [Government is] really getting to dangerous levels of complacency in [its] ability to look after our personal information.'

And the possibility for errors is enormous. 'By making ordinary life dependent on the reliability of a complex administrative system, the scheme makes myriad small errors potentially catastrophic,' points out No2ID.

'There's no hint from the government how it will deal with inevitably large numbers of misidentifications and errors, or deliberate attacks on or corruption of what would become a critical piece of national infrastructure.'

Parliament appears to have given the Home Secretary unlimited power to shape the register in the future and extend its coverage. There is limited oversight and no public scrutiny. The proposed National Identity Scheme Commissioner will not be reporting to Parliament and his powers are strictly limited.

The Home Secretary can cancel anyone's identity card or demand its surrender at any time. There is no right of appeal.

The Home Office estimates the cost of the ID card scheme at £6 billion but others believe the cost will be nearer £40 billion.

'The system offers a ready-made police state tool for a future government less trustworthy than the current one,' says No2ID. 'Welcome to a lifetime of State identity control.'

Roll up

THE Home Office says many people are impatient to receive their biometric identity cards and cannot wait until 2017. 'As I go around the country I regularly have people coming up to me and saying they don't want to wait that long,' Jacqui Smith said.

A special register has now been set up for anyone impatient for a place on the database. By signing up now, they can increase their chances of being among the first to be issued with a card.

People applying for a passport from 2010 will also be able to get an ID card early as the two will be issued together – so long as applicants pass the interview process.

Some 69 interview centres with 'biometric sampling facilities' have now been set up around the country. Compulsory interviews will be part of the process which the government itself admits will be 'intrusive'. These will include questions about previous employment, addresses and savings.

Under the government 'Action Plan', all ten 'fingerprint biometrics' will be recorded and stored in the National Identity Register. Iris scans are also envisaged.

Jacqui Smith confirmed talks are underway with private contractors to provide additional fingerprint and other biometric 'enrolment' services.

Ministers predict seven million people a year will apply for an identity card from 2012, in a market said to be worth £200 million a year. The biometric identity card comes with a starting price of around £60.

Papier bitte!

NEW LAWS to crackdown on illegal immigration make it an offence not to carry some form of identification. State officials now have the power to stop almost anyone and demand to see their papers. A refusal could lead to a year in jail or a £5,000 fine. Previously, such powers have only been used in time of war.

A clause within the Immigration and Citizenship Act 2009 allows officials to stop anyone they suspect of entering the country illegally. No reasonable cause or suspicion is required, and checks can be carried out 'in-country', not just at borders.

The only exception will be the minority of people who have never left the country, leading to claims that the government is targeting ethnic groups. The law has also been described as an attempt to introduce compulsory ID cards by the back door.

'Powers to examine identity documents, previously thought to apply only at ports of entry, will be extended to criminalise anyone in Britain who has ever left the country and fails to produce identity papers upon demand,' points out Liberty.

'We believe that the catch-all remit of this power is disproportionate and that its enactment would not only damage community relations but represent a fundamental shift in the relationship between the State and those present in the UK.'

Previously, police could only ask to see identity documents if they suspected a person had committed an offence.

Winston Churchill abolished ID papers for British citizens after the Second World War because the random police checks were deeply resented by the public.

Occupation: Terrorist

A QUARTER of Britons support Gordon Brown in his belief that a national ID card scheme will 'disrupt terrorists'. The former head of MI5, however, thinks they are 'absolutely useless' and a senior figure at GCHQ says the PM's claims are 'absolute bunkum'.

With forged ID cards already available on the internet and e-passports easily cloned, faith in the system is hard to find outside of government.

Former Home Secretary Jacqui Smith has held a lifelong desire to see Britons carry identification documents. 'I have always believed in the concept of a national identity scheme,' she explains. Both she and Gordon Brown promote the cards as a 'robust defence' in the war on terror.

But Harvey Mattinson, a senior IT consultant at GCHQ, the government's top secret listening station, said the claims were 'absolute bunkum', adding that the card's only use would be in sharing information between government departments.

'ID cards may be helpful in all kinds of things but I don't think they are necessarily going to make us any safer,' says Dame Stella Rimington, the former head of MI5. 'I don't think that anybody in the intelligence services, particularly in my former service, would be pressing for ID cards.'

Until a totally fool-proof system is devised, the cards risk compromise, she says. 'My angle on ID cards is that they may be of some use but only if they can be made unforgeable – and all our other documentation is quite easy to forge.'

An investigation by *The Times* revealed that the new micro-chipped e-passports, although said to be foolproof against identity theft, can be cloned and manipulated in minutes and accepted as genuine by the computer software recommended for use at international airports.

Home Office figures show that 5,400 fraudulent passports were 'probably' issued in 2007, around half the number of the previous year. The DVLA admits 'tens of thousands' of its licences are suspect. Figures uncovered by *The Guardian* show there may be around 100,000 'duplicate' driving licences in the system and nearly as many fictitious passports. 'The Home Office maintains the scale of the problem is impossible to quantify,' says the paper.

'No one has ever claimed ID cards are the complete answer to terrorism or crime but they will help tackle illegal working, money laundering, benefit fraud and terrorist activity,' insists the Home Office. 'Al-Qaeda's own training manual requires operatives to acquire false identities to hide their terrorist activities.'

Critics point out that Britain's apparent home-grown terrorists would, in time, have been issued with identity cards themselves.

As anti-card campaigner Mark Thomas points out: 'One-third of terrorists travel using multiple identities, cry the card's supporters. But they then fail to mention that two-thirds do not, because they use their own identities, and these people would have an ID card. For an ID card to stop terrorism, all terrorists would need to register for one, something they might not do.'

Not that this troubles Gordon Brown. Trust would appear to be a given. He counters arguments with rapier-like precision: 'Would most people not agree that if there are acceptable safeguards to protect civil liberties, there are advantages in a national identity scheme that could not just help us disrupt terrorists and criminals travelling on forged or stolen identities – but more fundamentally, protect each citizen's identity and prevent it being forged or stolen?'

Biometrics are for life

A COMMONS report warns that criminals may easily penetrate the National Identity Register and hijack a person's identity for ever.

'Once you start using biometrics on a very wide scale for all sorts of everyday transactions, the Mafia will also have your biometrics,' says the report's author, Ross Anderson, professor of security engineering at Cambridge University

'You don't know which shops are owned by the Mafia but if you end up having to put your fingerprint on the glass every time that you buy a can of Coke, sooner or later the Mafia will have the biometrics of millions of people.'

Flawed technology will simply play into the hands of criminals, he warns. Once the Mafia have a person's unique fingerprint data, they capture his or her identity forever.

'There is a fundamental security engineering problem with biometrics as opposed to the cryptographic keys in your chip and pin card,' he says. 'Biometric identity cards could be less secure as your details, such as fingerprints, cannot be changed if they are stolen.'

Many people with legitimate cause to conceal their identity or whereabouts may also be compromised. These include those fleeing domestic abuse; victims of 'honour' crimes; witnesses in criminal cases; those at risk of kidnapping; undercover investigators; people hounded by the Press; refugees from oppressive regimes; and terrorist targets.

'Once your biometrics become compromised, you cannot revoke them,' explains Professor Anderson. 'It is not practical to do eye or finger transplants.'

DATA: IS IT SAFE?

'It doesn't get much more personal than personal information and we should all be concerned at the potential for information to end up in the wrong hands or to be used for unforeseen purposes'
– Home Secretary Jacqui Smith (2007-2009).

THE government wants to store the personal details of every British citizen on the National Identity Register. Every recordable fact from school reports and diseases contracted to savings accounts and where the children go to school – even their unique genetic codes – will be linked and open to inspection. Thousands of State officials and their subcontractors will be allowed to probe our lives, along with a few overseas intelligence agencies and selected biotech industries.

Data Protection Act safeguards were swept aside under a clause tucked deep inside the Coroners and Justice Bill 2009 allowing any public body access to details held by every other government department, agency or council.

Previously, data protection restrictions required information to be used only for the purpose it was taken, such as limiting access to health records to the Department of Health. Now, even low-ranking council officials can access the most sensitive personal information, such as income, benefits, health records and certain police 'intelligence'.

Critics say the government has given a green light for medical records to be examined by the DVLC to identify drivers who pose a health risk, or school attendance data to be studied by the Department for Work and Pensions to verify parents' benefit claims.

Liberal Democrat justice spokesman David Howarth says it

is typical of the government to bury 'more building blocks of its surveillance State' in an Act to reform the coroner service.

According to Simon Davies of Privacy International, the new law will permit 'an almost limitless range of data sharing opportunities' both within government and between commercial firms.

It gives ministers the power to lay 'orders' before Parliament for the bulk disclosure of banking and telephone records to the BBC's television licensing agency and provide 'bulk provision of NHS and other medical files' to the insurance industry and medical research organisations, he says.

But Justice Secretary Jack Straw defends the exchange of personal data, saying people moving house will benefit because they only have to tell one public body.

'I think all members of the public are in two places on this. Data relating to you and your family should be protected and that is an absolute imperative,' he said. 'But you don't want personally to give the same information again and again if it can be safely held and safely transferred.'

While the government's figures show that on average one of its own computers is lost every day of the week and that over 300,000 people have their data go astray each month, Jacquie Smith says public support for the National Identity Register 'has remained broadly steady – at nearly 60 percent.'

'I am convinced that our increased awareness as a nation of the dangers of data loss and identity fraud makes the case for participation in the national identity scheme more pressing, rather than less,' she reassuringly explains.

'Rather than thinking of the State as an opponent of our liberties, set on thwarting our personal ambitions, in this context the role of government agencies is to defend our interests, to offer reassurance and trust, and to working in the most effective way possible to ease and to enable our lives.'

'This,' she says, 'is the argument that supports the principle of the national identity scheme.'

This is the argument

November 2007: HM Revenue and Customs loose two computer discs containing the UK's entire child benefit records including the personal details of 25 million people. The two discs contain the names, addresses, dates of birth, National Insurance numbers and bank account details of every person receiving child benefit.

December 2007: Details of three million candidates for the UK driving theory test go missing in the US Mid-West. Names, addresses and phone numbers are among the details stored on a computer hard drive belonging to a contractor working for the Driving Standards Agency.

Nine NHS trusts own up to losing confidential patient information. Hundreds of thousands of people are thought to be affected.

January 2008: A laptop with the details of 600,000 people hoping to join the Royal Navy, Royal Marines and the RAF is taken from a Naval officer's car in Birmingham. It contains passport numbers, National Insurance numbers and bank details.

April 2008: An Army officer looses his laptop when he pops out for a Big Mac. The MoD says the data is not sensitive and is fully encrypted. The apparent theft follows the tightening of rules on government employees taking their computers out of the office.

June 2008: A rail passenger finds highly sensitive intelligence papers about weapons of mass destruction in Iran, and Cabinet Office documents on Iraq and al-Qaeda stuffed between seats in a first class carriage. The seven-page 'UK Top Secret' file contains a report entitled 'Al-Qaeda Vulnerabilities' and an assessment of Iraq's security forces.

A computer disappears from Communities Secretary Hazel Blears' office containing constituency and government data on defence and 'extremism'. The department admits its officials had 'not fully' complied with guidance on handling sensitive data.

July 2008: The Ministry of Defence confirms that 121 computer memory sticks and 747 laptops have been lost or stolen in the past four years. But Armed Forces Minister Bob Ainsworth says 32 devices have been recovered.

A laptop with hospital records and personal details of 89 patients is stolen from Falkirk and District Royal Infirmary. The unencrypted data, including names, addresses and treatment details, had been kept in a cupboard.

August 2008: The Ministry of Justice owns up to the loss of records of 45,000 people. These include the dates of birth, National Insurance numbers, bank details and other information on 27,000 people providing 'services' to the department. A laptop also goes missing with detailed job applications from people applying for judicial positions within the service.

Confidential records and sensitive intelligence on tens of thousands of the country's most prolific criminals is lost in a major breach of security when data from the Police National Computer is downloaded by private contractor PA Consulting Group. This includes files on 33,000 serious offenders, 10,000 'priority criminals', and the names and dates of birth of every prisoner in England and Wales. There is also information on an unspecified number of people enlisted on drug intervention programmes.

A computer sold on eBay for £6.99 is found to hold the personal details of thousands of council tax payers. Bank account details and addresses are discovered on the hard drive. Other details include transcripts of conversations about householders' divorces and family bereavements.

Sensitive legal documents relating to a major drugs prosecution in Liverpool turn up on a refuse tip in Lancashire. The files relate to Operation Montrose which results in jail sentences for 59 men. They include more than 100 'restricted' statements from officers and forensic experts and the personal details of witnesses, including addresses.

September 2008: The government confirms that a portable hard drive holding details of up to 5,000 employees of the justice system – including prison staff – has been lost by private contractor EDS.

The Ministry of Defence launches an investigation into the theft of computer files containing the records of thousands of serving and former RAF staff. The breach is described as 'extremely serious' and a helpline for people affected is set up.

A digital camera containing MI6 images of terror suspects turns up on eBay. Faces, names and fingerprints, as well as pictures of rocket launchers and missiles, are discovered by an online bidder who buys the camera for £17.

October 2008: The Ministry of Defence report a computer hard drive missing. It contains the details of up to 1.7 million people, including the personal details of about 100,000 military personnel, 600,000 potential recruits, bank details, passport numbers, addresses, dates of birth, driving licence details and telephone numbers. The loss is discovered during an audit by IT contractor EDS.

A laptop with the personal details of 100,000 pensioners goes missing when an employee of the accountancy firm Deloitte has her handbag stolen. OAPs are warned that the loss of their names, addresses and National Insurance numbers could leave them vulnerable to ID fraudsters.

November 2008: A memory stick holding the private details of up to 12 million people along with the web passwords for a government computer system is found in a pub car park in Staffordshire. The Gateway website gives access to services including tax returns and child benefits. The memory stick was lost by an employee of subcontractor Atos Origin.

5

RESISTANCE IS FUTILE

'When I pass protestors every day at Downing Street – and believe me, you name it, they protest against it – I may not like what they call me, but I thank God they can. That's called freedom' – Tony Blair 2002.

TUCKED away inside the Serious Organised Crime and Police Act 2005 is 64-word clause which takes away our right to protest against the government – unless of course the police give permission first. This might seem strange in a democracy.

There is nothing new in having to inform the police of an upcoming demonstration – crowd control, public safety and traffic management need to be organised for the good of all. What is new is that the State will now organise the demonstration for you.

When Maya Evans and Milan Rai wanted to draw people's attention to the growing death toll in Iraq, they decided to read aloud the names of the war dead at London's Cenotaph. They did not get very far. They were quickly arrested by 14 police officers and bundled into a van.

Mr Rai became the first person in Britain to be jailed under the Act when he refused to pay fines totalling £600. They are both banned from entering any area that the police choose to 'designate'.

'I just think it's a shame that you can't voice your freedom of speech in this country any more and it is illegal to hold a remembrance ceremony for the dead,' said Ms Evans, 25, from Hastings.

Section 132 was quietly slipped into an Act of Parliament designed to disrupt seriously organised criminals because Tony Blair and others were annoyed that one man – anti-war protester Brian Haw – could protest on their doorstep and that they were powerless to stop him.

Section 132 says: *Any person who organises a demonstration in a public place in the designated area, or takes part in a demonstration in a public place in the designated area, or carries on a demonstration by himself in a public place in the designated area, is guilty of an offence if, when the demonstration starts, authorisation for the demonstration has not been given under section 134.*

The police require six days notice. Anyone flouting the new law faces 51 weeks imprisonment or a £2,500 fine.

'It had always been practice to book a slot to protest anywhere near Downing Street. This was for obvious safety and practical reasons relating to the police being able to organise groups of people,' explains Ms Evans. 'I don't object to this practical procedure.

'SOCPA, however, is very different to the old procedure. This piece of legislation allows the police to effectively shape your protest. This, in effect, means in order to protest against the State you have to allow your protest to be designed by the State in terms of location, numbers, visibility, noise and length of time.'

Liberal Democrat Peer Baroness Miller says the law has had a 'chilling' effect on people, leading them to believe that demonstrations are banned.

'Freedom to demonstrate outside Parliament is one of the most important freedoms of expression that Britain has,' she says. 'This government changed that fundamental freedom to a conditional one. Now people are afraid they will get a criminal record for simply holding a placard or even wearing a T-shirt in the environs of Parliament,' she said.

When members of the House of Lords wanted to protest in the 'exclusion zone' by reading aloud a list of those arrested under the Act, they found themselves in the ridiculous position of having to ask the police for permission.

'It comes to something when Parliamentarians can't even protest outside their own House without say-so from the police,' said a Liberal Democrat spokesman.

The original 'designated area' covers a one-kilometre zone around Parliament Square. However, the police are free to name anywhere a 'designated area' to prevent protest. So far, the Women's Peace Camp at Aldermaston – Britain's atomic weapons establishment – has been declared a no-protest zone, as has the world's largest secret listening station at Menwith Hill in Yorkshire, run by the US National Security Agency.

Other areas subsequently named 'designated areas' include royal palaces and government buildings. No justification for designation is required.

'So this piece of legislation isn't just about the area around Parliament,' points out Ms Evans. 'It has the potential to be expanded to every government building in this country. If we don't demand its repeal, we may see the day when we can't freely protest outside our own town halls.'

The police have additional powers to break up any protest or demonstration under Section 30 of the Anti-Social Behaviour Act 2003 if a senior police officer has reasonable grounds to believe any member of the public has been 'intimidated, harassed, alarmed or distressed'. The law applies to groups of two or more persons.

'Any situation where the police are able to self authorise restrictions on the right to protest should be treated with great caution,' points out Liberty. 'These powers give rise to criminal sanction for behaviour that would not in itself be unlawful. The government – with no given justification – has decided that two people can constitute an assembly.'

Shoppers and office-workers were threatened with arrest when they witnessed police confiscating free speech leaflets at an event in Liverpool to mark 'Freedom Not Fear 2008', the international action day for civil liberties.

'Disgusted passers-by quickly became involved,' said local man Adam Ford. 'Shouts of "you're a disgrace" and "free speech" could be heard. Around a dozen forceful police eventually made two arrests.'

An amendment to SOCPA brought in under the Serious Crime Act 2007 criminalises people who are 'intentionally encouraging or assisting an offence'. They face the same penalties as event organisers.

'Bollocks to Blair'

POLICE moved in quickly when they spotted a young woman wearing a T-shirt bearing an anti-government slogan at a country fair in Shropshire. Charlotte Denis, 20, was ordered to remove her top because the words 'Bollocks to Blair' were deemed 'offensive.'

She says she was shocked at their heavy-handed tactics. 'What do you want me to do?' she asked. 'Take my top off and wear my bra?'

She was then frogmarched to a waiting police car. 'They grabbed me as if I was a football hooligan,' she says. 'I asked the officers how they could arrest someone for wearing a T-shirt and they told me it was because it would offend old people.'

Two British Transport Police officers threatened a local Conservative party campaigner with arrest when she handed out leaflets on the London Underground. Julia Gobert happened to be wearing a jacket with an anti-Blair slogan.

Leicestershire market trader Tony Wright, 60, was given an £80 fixed penalty fine for selling clothes with anti-government slogans. Police said the words could 'cause alarm or distress'.

'I am a local country boy,' said Mr Wright. 'I don't see anything wrong with me expressing my opinion about Blair. The ticket is a joke.'

Eighty-year-old peace campaigner John Catt was stopped by police officers as a 'terrorist suspect' for wearing a T-shirt with anti-Blair and Bush slogans.

Mr Catt, who served with the RAF in the Second World War, was stopped and searched by police in Brighton and made to sign a form confirming he had been interviewed under the Terrorism Act 2000.

The official record confirms that the 'purpose' of the search was 'terrorism' and the 'grounds for intervention' were 'carrying plackard and T-shirt with anti-Blair info' (sic).

Flag burners 'inflame'

THE POLICE want extra powers to arrest people who burn flags – making it a new criminal offence. They say the public wants to see action against Islamic 'extremists' and others preaching violence and religious hate.

The plans, drawn up by Scotland Yard and submitted to the Attorney General Lord Goldsmith, urge the government to ban demonstrators from covering their faces to avoid police scrutiny. They also want tougher powers to arrest demonstrators who 'inflame tensions'.

'There appears to be a growing public perception that policing of demonstrations is unduly lenient,' said the Assistant Commissioner Tarique Ghaffur in 2006. 'That view was shared by law-abiding citizens of all backgrounds.'

He also called for new powers to allow the police to vet placards and banners and remove those deemed 'offensive'.

The Straw pledge

VETERAN peace campaigner Walter Wolfgang, 82, was physically ejected from New Labour's annual conference in 2005 when he used the word 'nonsense' to describe Foreign Secretary Jack Straw's explanation for the Iraq invasion.

Mr Wolfgang, who escaped Nazi Germany in 1937, was prevented from returning to the conference by police using powers under the Terrorism Act 2000.

He called out the word when Mr Straw told delegates: 'We are in Iraq for one reason only – to help the elected Iraqi government build a secure, democratic and stable nation.'

A shaken Mr Wolfgang – a member of the Labour Party for 57 years – spoke to reporters outside. 'These two toughies came round and wanted to manhandle me out. They were trying to pull me out. I refused to let them.'

Delegates sitting nearby were heard to call out 'Shame' and 'Leave him alone' as the pensioner was dragged from his seat.

Steve Forrest, chairman of Erith Thamesmead Labour party, who protested at Mr Wolfgang's treatment, was bundled out more forcefully after telling stewards: 'You must be joking.'

At the other end of the age spectrum, Isabelle Ellis-Cockcroft, 11, was issued with a stop-and-search notice under Section 44 of the Terrorism Act 2000 when she accompanied her father on a visit to the peace camp at RAF Fairford in Gloucestershire.

Isabelle told the BBC: 'They asked what was in our pockets, wrote down our descriptions and checked a backpack and a bike we had with us. They said they were stopping us under the Terrorism Act, but I'm not a terrorist.'

Her father, David, said he tried to reason with police when they wanted to search her. 'I argued against them searching her and told them it was patently absurd,' he said.

In all, more than 1,000 people were stopped and searched on the day. Police also took it upon themselves to turn back three coaches containing CND members, Quakers and a samba band. The buses were escorted directly back to London by a police convoy.

When the Terrorism Act was debated in the Commons in December 1999, Jack Straw, then Home Secretary, said: 'The Bill does not focus on demonstrations, which are a normal activity in a democracy. I wholly defend people's right to go in for peaceful protest.'

Police ban anti-war camp

THE government was accused of censorship when it banned a peace camp from pitching tents near New Labour's annual conference in Manchester. Police cited health and safety reasons and an increased terror alert.

Around 20 people from Military Families Against The War had planned to pitch tents in Albert Square in front of the Town Hall.

Rose Gentle from Glasgow, whose 19-year-old son Gordon died in Iraq, accused the police and local Labour council of 'doing the government's bidding'.

'We think it's because it's the Labour conference and they don't want us going and voicing our opinions because Mr Blair is going to be there,' she said.

'They say it's health and safety. They said they don't want drunks thinking it's somewhere they can sleep. But we've got our own security.'

Assistant Chief Constable Stephen Thomas of Greater Manchester Police defended what he termed 'robust policing' that prevented anyone entering an 'exclusion zone' around the conference.

'There is no specific threat to Manchester at the moment,' he explained. 'But obviously the UK's national threat level is currently severe.'

Police block Post Office march

POLICE used health and safety laws to halt a protest march against the closure of a local Post Office. Although the residents of Altarnun in Cornwall are now expected to travel four miles to their nearest alternative, the journey was deemed 'too risky' for the 200 marchers.

The villagers had planned to walk to nearby Lewannick Post Office but police stepped in to halt the protest after they had travelled just one mile.

Parish clerk Peter Allen was told to turn back the group or

disperse because the busy A30 posed an 'extreme risk of injury'.

Opponents of the closure argue that with an infrequent bus service they will be obliged to walk the four miles to Lewannick or else take a 16-mile round trip by car.

St George pays price of protest

PUPILS protesting against the closure of their school learnt an interesting lesson in civics when they were landed with a £2,500 bill by the very council trying to close them down.

Salford City Council had earlier halted another protest by pupils at the town hall by citing an obscure law that prevents council property being used for protests in the run-up to an election.

The girls of St George's RC High School in Salford have been fighting a long-running battle to halt the closure of their popular and successful school under the government's Building Schools for the Future project.

But when they held a protest march, attended by 1,000 pupils, parents and well-wishers, the council charged them for the cost of closing roads, controlling traffic lights and putting out cones. The money was taken directly from the school's bank account.

'They've just gone ahead and taken the money from our account. It shows the callousness of the council,' said headteacher Phil Harte. 'I think it's appalling that when you protest against the council you have to pay for the right to do that.'

The girls were forced to cancel another protest when they attempted to mark St George's Day by dressing a teaching assistant as their school's namesake. She planned to ride a horse to Swinton Civic Centre and hand out red roses to councillors.

The town hall's legal team where quick to nip the protest in the bud. Solicitor Anthony Rich wrote to say that, as the school closure was a 'politically controversial issue', the council was duty-bound to ban them from council grounds under the Local Government Act 1986.

The ban was justified, said Mr Rich, because: 'This issue was not as simple as students wishing to celebrate St George's Day at the town hall but was quite clearly intended to be part of the school's campaign against its proposed closure.'

'We're incandescent with rage,' said Heather Ennis of the Justice4Georges campaign. 'Twenty-two-thousand police marched in London and they didn't get charged a penny!'

'They're trying to stop us because we're kids and we're fighting against their proposals. I don't think it's fair at all.'

Police crush tank stunt

PLANS to highlight the lack of equipment provided to British soldiers serving in Iraq and Afghanistan were crushed when Lancashire police broke up a protest organised by a Conservative splinter group.

Conservative Way Forward had planned to drive a tank through Blackpool with a group of supporters dressed as poorly-equipped servicemen but police were quick to advance on the town's Talbot Square.

They ordered that the demonstration be broken up and that the tank – an Abbott self-propelled gun – withdraw to less contentious ground.

'The police seemed to be behaving in a heavy-handed manner,' one eyewitness told the *Daily Telegraph*. 'A police van and a couple more police vehicles were involved, and at least a dozen officers were at the scene. One of them was filming what was happening with a video camera for "evidence gathering".'

The Northampton-based company that supplied the vehicle, Tanks-a-Lot, said it was perfectly road-legal. 'It is properly taxed, insured and registered,' explained Nick Mead. 'It's not that it's not allowed on the roads.'

'I'm disappointed that we were not allowed to drive around Blackpool,' said event organiser Mark Allatt. 'British soldiers have died in Afghanistan and Iraq because they were sent into action without body armour or asked to patrol in vehicles which didn't have adequate armour.'

Curtains for demo film

THE police are stopping venues around the country from screening an independent film that shows them in a bad light. 'On the Verge' documents the long-running campaign against a Brighton weapons factory and cost just £500 to make.

The film's début screening at Brighton's Duke of York cinema was cancelled when police insisted the private showing to just 12 people required certification from the British Board of Film Classification.

Other venues across the country – including Southampton, Chichester, Bath and Oxford – have been pressured by police to cancel screenings, say the film's makers.

'I am extremely disappointed but not entirely surprised by the police's action,' said Steven Bishop of SchMovies.

'If the police really had problems over the certificate they could have approached us at a much earlier stage,' he said. 'Our film – although focussing mainly on the rights and wrongs of protest – shows a number of examples of questionable police behaviour. Perhaps this is why they left their move so late.'

A spokesperson for the Sussex force confirmed that the police had intervened in the showing. 'A junior officer who is not based in the city alerted the city council to the showing and they advised the cinema of its responsibilities,' he said.

Staff at the Arthouse Community Cafe in Southampton were told to pull the documentary by police and licensing officers. Director Jani Franck said: 'I grew up in South Africa and this feels awfully familiar. This has nothing to do with protecting the public. This is nothing but censorship.'

WATCHING THE REPORTERS

'It is for the local Chief Constable…to decide how his or her officers and employees should best balance the rights to freedom of the Press, freedom of expression and the need for public protection'
– Home Secretary Jacqui Smith (2007-2009).

PRESS photographer Marc Vallée had to be taken to hospital by ambulance after police decided he should not take pictures of protestors outside Parliament. The highly respected photojournalist had been covering the Sack Parliament demonstration when officers decided public protection was paramount before throwing him to the ground.

As soon as he was bundled out of the way, the police cordoned off the demonstration – kettling protestors and Press.

'Several journalists were inside the police ring and, when finally allowed to leave, were forced to give their names and address and show proof of ID in order to receive a possible summons for the offence of attending an unlawful protest,' one reporter told the National Union of Journalists (NUJ) magazine *The Freelance*.

'It seems that journalists going about their lawful business of newsgathering are being treated like protesters under the clause of the Serious Organised Crime and Police Act,' says the union, which wants clarification that journalists doing their job should not be subject to SOCPA.

The NUJ's general secretary, Jeremy Dear, says it is 'disgraceful that the police brutally obstructed a member of the Press from reporting on a political demonstration'.

'Press freedom is a central tenet of our democracy so Marc Vallée's treatment by the police is deeply worrying,' he says.

'Neither the Commissioner of the Metropolitan Police or his officers has any legal power, moral responsibility or political responsibility to prevent or restrict what the media record,' says

Marc Vallée's solicitor, Chez Cotton.

In April 2008, Labour MP Austin Mitchell led a delegation of photographers to the Home Office to protest at police harassment and at an apparent ban on taking pictures in public places.

'People have complained about photographers being stopped from taking pictures by police, PCSOs, wardens and by various officious people,' said Mr Mitchell.

'People have a right to take photographs; and to start interfering with that is crazy. It seems crazy when the streets are festooned with closed-circuit television cameras that the public should be stopped from using cameras.'

The number of complaints against the police for Press harassment has risen steadily over the years. David Hoffman, a freelance with more than 30 years experience, told another NUJ publication, *The Journalist*: 'I was taking pictures of the party on the London tube – the last day people could drink alcohol – from a good distance when two police officers started pushing me around and put a hand over my lens.'

'There was no reason at all. I was simply recording the event and they stopped me because they thought they could. That's a very typical incident. That will happen to me once a week if I'm out working.'

Guidelines drawn up between the Association of Chief Police Officers and media groups are routinely ignored. The NUJ says the police regularly stop the filming of interviews under the Prevention of Terrorism Act 2000 and hold journalists in police custody for obstruction, despite a clear commitment not to hinder reporters.

Under the agreement, it was confirmed that the Press do not need permits to film in public and that the police have no power to restrict what is recorded. They should also help the media carry out its duty to report from the scene of an incident.

'Most officers don't even look at the guidelines, don't know what they are, and probably don't care about them,' says Jeff Moore, chairman of the British Press Photographers' Association.

'I was speaking to a police inspector at Westminster who'd just been on a media training course and didn't know about any guidelines.'

Reporters also complain of a sinister form of intimidation by police Forward Intelligence Teams (FIT), a unit originally tasked with recording anti-social behaviour and public disorder.

The NUJ reports that FIT units have started surveillance of members and says journalists and photographers are logged with a four-figure 'photographic reference number' on the police database.

When Jeremy Dear complained to Home Secretary Jacqui Smith of 'intimidatory policing', he was able to cite examples of police officers who knew journalists by name, and followed and filmed them while working.

He says every single journalist covering a demonstration outside Parliament against restrictions in the Serious Organised Crime and Police Act was catalogued by FIT.

Shoot the messenger

THE CROWN Prosecution Service tried to have a journalist jailed for receiving information off-the-record from a police officer. But Sally Murrer walked free after the judge ruled Thames Valley force had broken European laws that protect the rights of journalists and their sources.

Ms Murrer – a reporter on the Milton Keynes *Citizen* newspaper accused of obtaining police information illegally – was freed when prosecution evidence obtained from secret bugging was deemed inadmissible.

Thames Valley Police had secretly recorded conversations between the reporter and former detective sergeant Mark Kearney in his car. Ms Murrer was accused of three offences of aiding and abetting misconduct in a public office.

'It's been a very long, horrible, nasty and vindictive case and we are all exhausted,' said Ms Murrer after the trial was halted. 'We have done all emotions over the last 19 months, now it's just about survival.'

NUJ general secretary Jeremy Dear said: 'This case was yet another example of members of the police force believing they were above the law, able to trample over well-established journalistic rights and freedoms.'

'Let's be clear, this was an attempt to make a criminal out of a journalist for receiving information that the State didn't want to get out. It was a misguided prosecution that sought to punish Sally for simply doing her job.'

Her solicitor, Louis Charalambous, said Thames Valley police had trampled on legal safeguards for the protection of journalists 'when they chose to bug Sally's conversations under a warrant that failed to mention that she was a journalist, and later when she was arrested and brought to a police station where, following a strip search and a night in the cells, she faced a gruelling interrogation – while her home and office were searched, and all of her notebooks seized.'

'Had the case against Sally gone ahead, it would have signalled a lurch towards a police state, a situation which is abhorrent in the minds of right thinking people,' he said.

Blanket ban

TV NEWS crews and Press photographers will be banned from recording demonstrations and public unrest if they risk photographing police officers in the process. Section 76 of the Counter-Terrorism Act 2008 – intended to protect the identity of military and security personnel – makes it a criminal offence to take pictures of the police.

The law has been roundly condemned. The National Union of Journalists and the British Press Photographers' Association say the Act extends powers that are already used to harass photographers and are yet a further erosion of Press freedom.

Under Section 76, eliciting, publishing or communicating

information on members of the armed forces, intelligence services and police officers which is 'likely to be useful to a person committing or preparing an act of terrorism' will be an offence carrying a maximum jail term of 10 years.

Photographer Marc Vallée believes the new powers are too vague to prevent abuse. 'I can see it now,' he says. 'If you don't stop taking pictures of me hitting this protester on the head, I'm going to nick you under section 76 of the Counter-Terrorism Act 2008.'

The minister for policing, crime and security, Vernon Coaker, previously warned the media that photography could be limited 'on the grounds of national security, or there may be situations in which the taking of photographs may cause or lead to public order situations or inflame an already tense situation or raise security considerations', he said.

'Additionally, the police may require a person to move on in order to prevent a breach of the peace or to avoid a public order situation or for the person's own safety and welfare or for the safety and welfare of others.'

'I have to say I find the 'for your own safety and welfare' line a bit hard to swallow,' says Vallée. 'Documenting political dissent in Britain is under attack and just in time for the political and industrial fall out from the recession.'

'The right to take photos in a public place is a precious freedom,' insists the NUJ's Jeremy Dear. 'It is what enables the Press to show the wider world what is going on.'

A Home Office spokesperson said it will be up to individual officers how they interpret the law.

Gagging orders
NEWSPAPERS and television could be banned from reporting on 'national security' matters if plans being drawn up by the cross-party Intelligence and Security Committee receive approval from Gordon Brown.

The Independent quotes unnamed Whitehall sources as saying the

ISC is also recommending censorship in the reporting of police operations with national security implications.

Unlike other Westminster committees, the ISC is appointed by Prime Minister Gordon Brown, rather than Parliament, and reports direct to him.

Critics say any such ban on reporting represents a fundamental shift in the relationship between the Press and the State.

'This would be a very dangerous development. We need media scrutiny for public accountability,' says human rights lawyer Louise Christian. 'We can see this from the example, for instance, of the PhD student in Nottingham who was banged up for six days without charge because he downloaded something from the internet for his thesis.'

'The only reason this came to light was because of the media attention to the case.'

WHEN RESEARCH IS A CRIME

'Everyone has the right to freedom of opinion and expression; this right includes freedom to hold opinions without interference and to seek, receive and impart information and ideas through any media and regardless of frontiers' – Universal Declaration of Human Rights.

DURING his six days in police custody, Rizwaan Sabir says he was subjected to a form of sleep deprivation which he describes as 'psychological torture'. 'I was absolutely broken. I didn't sleep. I'd close my eyes then hear the keys clanking and I would be up again.'

At first, Sabir, 22, thought he was on the receiving end of a practical joke. He had earlier asked a friend to print out a lengthy document downloaded from the US Justice Department website.

'Are you having a laugh?' he asked the officers who came to

take him away. 'I was absolutely baffled. I just could not believe it.'

He also found it hard to believe that staff at Nottingham University had been trawling through his friend's computer files. A spokesperson for the university said they had a duty to inform police when they discovered the document, said to be the official al Qaeda training manual.

Sabir and his friend – university administrator Hisham Yezza – were arrested on the spot and held for the best part of a week, despite statements from tutors that the document was directly relevant to Sabir's research for his master's degree in international relations.

The men were separated and Sabir was held in a sealed off prison wing and placed under 24-hour surveillance. 'I have never been that low in my life,' he said. 'I did not sleep for six days. I thought I was going to end up as a Category A prisoner in Belmarsh. It absolutely broke me. I was sitting there crying.'

For the first 48 hours, police refused to explain why he was being held. He was interrogated daily about his views on al Qaeda, Islamic literature and fellow students.

'Six days felt like six years. I dread to think what 42 days would feel like: 28 days is harsh enough. The idea of 42 days is phenomenal,' he told *The Guardian*. 'The ironic thing is, paedophiles, murderers, bank robbers, kidnappers and extortionists are held for four days – 96 hours maximum time.'

The young PhD student had been a popular and active figure on the campus. He was general secretary of the International Students' Bureau and a founder of the student peace movement. He was also personal assistant to the head of modern languages. He is sorry nobody bothered to ask him about the document before calling in the police.

'Someone could be forgiven in this current climate for panicking at this type of document,' he says. 'But I would have appreciated had I been given five minutes simply to answer the questions relevant to the document. Once the procedure was launched it was quickly out of the university's hands.'

Although both men were later released without charge, Yezza was subsequently re-arrested and held in detention prior to possible deportation to Algeria.

'If he is taken to Algeria, he may be subjected to severe human rights violations after his involvement in this case,' says Dr Alf Nilsen, a research fellow at the university's school of politics and international relations. 'He has been in the UK for 13 years. His work is here, his friends are here, his life is here.'

Their arrest has been described by lecturers as a direct assault on academic freedom. The government, they say, is putting pressure on academics to become police informers.

'It's a very, very worrying trend that needs to be opposed, this mindset that views everything with extreme suspicion,' says Sabir. 'No intellectual progress takes place without a sense of curiosity, without a sense of going beyond what we know already, beyond the established facts and notions and truths; that's how scientific and intellectual revolutions have been achieved.'

Students and lecturers at Nottingham say the arrests have been taken as a clear message from the police 'that they are likely to arrest those who have been engaged in peaceful political activities'.

In a joint statement, they warned: 'The overt police presence on campus, combined with increased and intimidating police presence at recent peaceful demonstrations, has created a climate of fear amongst some students.'

'There is widespread concern in the community that the police are criminalising peaceful activists using terrorism legislation.'

Dr Nilsen says the pervading climate of fear amounts to an assault not just on academic freedom but on intellectual freedom as a whole. 'What does this say about people's right to inform themselves about issues of public concern? It says something about the potential implications of being politically active on campus in a time when a culture of fear merges with draconian terror legislation.'

Early in 2008, the Court of Appeal quashed the convictions of two Rochdale men earlier jailed for three years for their part in a

Bradford University 'ring' that downloaded 'extremist material'. During their trial at the Old Bailey they argued that they were not terrorists but intellectually curious.

Lawyers for Aitaz Zafar, 21, and Awaab Iqbal, 20, argued at London's Appeal Court that the material in their possession was mere 'propaganda' and they said the 'maverick' decision to prosecute had violated their human rights to freedom of thought, conscience, religion and expression.

Maroof Shaffi, who teaches at Bradford, says the heightened security situation and anti-terror laws are leaving many Muslims students in fear of arrest.

'I was doing some research and I suddenly looked at the titles of the books that I was buying and every book had the word *Jihad* in it,' he says. 'It pricked my conscience a bit, that somebody would somehow see these books as being those kind of books kept in the house of a violent extremist.'

Many are worried at the long-term effect these arrests will have on academic research and debate. 'What worries me is this self-censorship and gradual erosion of our academic freedom,' says Catherine Pope, a lecturer at Southampton University. 'Before we know it, we will be self-censoring and will not be able to change it.'

DON'T BANK ON THE INTERNET

'Where there is illegal material on the net, I want it removed' – Home Secretary Jacqui Smith (2007-2009).

WHEN Google joined forces with the Chinese government to censor internet content there was uproar. When similar moves were introduced in Britain the response was somewhat mooted.

Today, the State has unlimited power to restrict what we read and watch on-line. The police can call for a website to be taken down or have its access blocked if they suspect the content in any way 'glorifies' terrorism.

Tools used to track down and close child pornographers are being used with success against other content deemed 'extreme' by police and government officials.

Internet service providers (ISPs) receive regular lists of sites to be blocked under a system known as Cleanfeed. The list is drawn up by the Internet Watch Foundation – whose original remit was to tackle child pornography – and added to by the Home Office with the instruction 'block traffic to and from these addresses'.

The system was adopted voluntarily by all UK ISPs in December 2007. Those who do not comply face charges of disseminating 'extremist' material.

'There is growing evidence people may be using the internet both to spread messages and to plan specifically for terrorism,' says Jacqui Smith. 'That is why, as well as changing the law to make sure we can tackle that, there is more we need to do to show the internet is not a no-go area as far as tackling terrorism is concerned.'

But critics warn of the lack of oversight, stressing that very few people actually know what is being blocked.

'We're led to believe that it's purely a list of child pornography sites,' says *Guardian* columnist Frank Fisher. 'But no one outside government knows. Not even the ISPs. They block; they don't look.'

In his on-line column, Fisher told his readers: 'You're now viewing a State-mandated subset of the internet. How do you feel about that? Like to vote against it? You can't. Like your MP to sit on a committee to oversee implementation? He can't. Like to know if the Google results you're seeing are a full representation of Google's actual results? You can't,' he told them.

'Censorship at this level – above even ISPs – is all but invisible to the end user. It's a secret that they're keeping these secrets from you.'

Closing down the critics

WHEN pensioner James Hulbert posted an open letter to the Lord Chancellor Lord Irvine on the internet claiming he had been denied justice in a series of court cases, the head of the judiciary was quick to see that justice was done. He had the website taken down.

The letter charted a nine-year battle to win redress in the courts after being acquitted of charges of deception. In it, Mr Hulbert, 67, described what he called 'his outrageous treatment at the hands of the courts and the police' and he named five judges.

Within days, Lord Irvine's department wrote to Mr Hulbert's local service provider – Kingston Internet Webmaster – describing the complaints against the judges and police as 'offensive' and demanding instant removal. Mr Hulbert said he had been asserting his right to free speech.

Yaman Akdeniz, director of CyberRights and CyberLiberties, says this is a case of political pressure being brought to bear on ISPs.

'Receiving a letter from the Lord Chancellor is bound to have a significant impact on any ISP. He is using his political position to pressurise Kingston.'

In an earlier case, a judge ruled that ISPs and hosting companies are liable for 'offensive' material posted on the internet in the same way a newspaper is responsible for its content. He also ruled that 'offensive' material must be removed if the ISP receives notice of its existence – a judgement obliging ISPs to become censors.

Justice Morland ruled in the case of Laurence Godfrey versus Demon Internet that libellous comments about Mr Godfrey posted on a chat-room site were the responsibility of Demon.

'ISPs are scared and many don't have the legal departments of Demon or AOL,' says Mr Akdeniz. 'What can they do? They are bound to take material down.'

The police stepped in to have a Facebook page closed down when one of their own was accused of being 'too officious' while 'persecuting motorists' in Sudbury, Suffolk.

Police said comments by more than 1,000 locals angered at the Police Community Support Officer's zealous manner were 'offensive'.

A spokesperson for Suffolk police confirmed: 'A request was made to a social networking site to remove some inappropriate messages about one of Suffolk Constabulary's employees.'

Combing the Web

PLANS are afoot to install an array of 'black box probes' throughout Britain's communications network to log every single internet visit, every email and on-line chat – together with phone calls and texts. The details will then be stored in Britain's biggest database, allowing police and security agents to trawl through the mass of our communications in search of crimes.

The blandly-named Interception Modernisation Programme promises to dwarf even the National Identity Register to qualify as the most costly data-collection exercise in UK history. Even its budget is top secret.

'Given the commercial and national security sensitivities,' said Home Secretary Jacqui Smith, 'The precise costs of the programme cannot be disclosed.'

Some estimates put the cost at around £12 billion although it is hoped to economise by involving the private sector in data collection.

From his office within the government's eavesdropping agency in Cheltenham, GCHQ director Sir David Pepper is overseeing the plan to insert thousands of 'live taps' into the heart of our communications network and then route our personal correspondence direct to his database.

He believes that only a vast central database can cope with the array of communications between terrorists planning attacks on Britain, and he says emails and on-line chats are the preferred methods of communication between al Qaeda operatives.

The Home Office says it can no longer rely on ISPs to store the information for them in a world of ever-increase data traffic. They were legally compelled to do so in March 2009. Now it says the growing terror threat requires a more robust effort to not only gather data but to analyse it as well.

And, although the Home Office says intercepted communications have been used as evidence in 95 percent of serious crime cases and almost all security service operations since 2004, it insists even more powers are needed.

Ms Smith says the Interception Modernisation Programme will 'ensure that our capability to lawfully intercept and exploit data when fighting crime and terrorism is not lost' and she promised to introduce strict guidelines to ensure personal privacy in the 'spirit of openness and accountability'.

But Sir Ken Macdonald, Director of Public Prosecutions from 2003 to 2008, says the project is 'a paranoid fantasy which would destroy everything that makes living worthwhile'.

The former barrister had earlier clashed with the Home Secretary when he insisted there was 'no war on terror', warning that the government's 'fear-driven and inappropriate' response was putting Britain's due process of law in serious jeopardy.

'We must avoid surrendering our freedom as autonomous human beings to such an ugly future. We should make judgments that are compatible with our status as free people,' he says. 'This database would be an unimaginable hell-house of personal private information.'

'It would be a complete readout of every citizen's life in the most intimate and demeaning detail. No government of any colour is to be trusted with such a roadmap to our souls.'

SECTION 60: 'EMPTY YOUR POCKETS'

The feedback, the very limited complaints and the public reaction to the

way we go about using this power shows that we're not misusing it
overall or in specific cases' – Commander Simon Bray, head of
Metropolitan Police stop and search policy.

POLICE are using the knife crime 'epidemic' to stop and search
people at random. A range of laws – some old and others specific
to the blade menace – sanction body searches on the public even
if officers do not suspect any weapons are being concealed. The
extra police powers are being turned against peaceful protestors
and are having little effect on would-be killers.

Forces across Britain have dusted down an old law that allows
officers to search for weapons or dangerous instruments 'whether
or not the officer has any grounds for suspecting that the person
or vehicle is carrying such articles'. Section 60 of the Criminal
Justice and Public Order Act 1994 was originally intended to
counter football hooligans.

Commander Mark Simmons of Scotland Yard says the old law
has proved to be an 'absolutely key tactic' in the fight against knife
crime. 'We think we are on the right track,' he explains when he
says police in London have conducted 157,000 Section 60 searches
in just over a year, resulting in 1,200 arrests.

A senior officer can 'designate' any area subject to the Section
60 search powers. To date, these have included peace camps, power
plants, detention centres and Heathrow airport. Anyone caught in
a 'designated' area can be stopped and searched without the police
having to give a reason.

Additionally, police already have the power to stop and search
anybody in a 'designated' area under Section 44 of the Terrorism
Act 2000.

'We need to be very careful about this,' says Dr Marian
Fitzgerald, a leading criminologist at the University of Kent. She
fears the new tactics will lead to unrest and points to the Brixton
riots in 1980 which were sparked by 'excessive' searching.

She says the move has minimal effect on crime, with police

coming away empty-handed 97 times out of a hundred, and she questions how such powers could come to be used routinely.

'Section 60 only allows them to be used in a designated place for 24 hours extending up to 36 hours in exceptional circumstances. I have not heard any explanation from the Met police how they now believe it is possible to use them on an almost permanent basis across 10 London boroughs,' she said.

Police armed with 'search wands' are now a common sight in the capital as are 'knife arches' that allow officers to randomly search passers-by for weapons. Anybody refusing to be searched faces arrest and having their details, including DNA, logged on the police national computer, together with a £1,000 fine or a month in jail.

Official figures show complaints against random searches rose by nearly a quarter in 2008, with a total for England and Wales of 536. Of these, just 169 received further investigation, with the IPCC concluding that 88 percent of complaints were 'unfounded'.

Graphic stories of knife crimes and their victims – given priority treatment by the police – have helped fuel demands for wider powers to deal with the menace. Even senior judges have climbed aboard the bandwagon.

The president of the High Court Queen's Bench Division echoed politicians, leader-writers and the public in demanding 'zero tolerance'. Sir Igor Judge says knife crime is an 'escalating and grave' problem. 'Offences of this kind are reaching epidemic proportions,' he told *The Sun*.

Curiously, during the peak of the 'epidemic' when the Metropolitan Police said knives posed a greater threat to young Londoners than terrorists, the force's own website was showing a 13.1 percent *drop* in knife crime. The Home Office has also been heavily criticised for releasing 'selective' figures to justify the increased police search powers.

Staff at the UK Statistics Authority are said to have 'pleaded' with Home Office officials not to release data before it had been thoroughly checked and confirmed.

Sir Michael Scholar, who heads the Authority, accused the Home Office and No 10 of breaking their own rules by putting out 'unchecked' and 'selective' data to build the case for further powers.

'There is a code designed to prevent political manipulation and my authority was set up to police this code. I am sorry to say the Home Office and No 10 broke these rules.'

Not letting the facts get in the way of a good story, the Home Secretary has been quick to launch a number of 'initiatives', including the Tackling Knives Action Programme, the Violent Crime Action Plan, and Operations Blunt 1 and 2 which, in addition to beefed up search powers, include authorisation for an increase in covert surveillance and 'targeted multi-agency crackdowns'.

Jacqui Smith insists these new measures are 'making a real difference on the ground' but says much more remains to be done.

Off with the fetters

ANYONE using public transport in London will automatically be giving their consent to a police frisking under proposals being considered by the Home Office.

British Transport Police say they want to change the rail 'conditions of carriage' to close a 'loophole' that prevents officers searching people without 'reasonable suspicion'.

Currently, police must invoke terror or anti-hooligan laws if they wish to search people at random.

Transport police told MPs: 'In effect, a suspect may not be searched, even where consent is provided, in an absence of "reasonable suspicion"; a procedural stumbling block to the unfettered use of knife arches.'

In with the shields

A FAMILY day out for climate change campaigners turned sour

when police sent in the riot squad and designated a vast area of Yorkshire farmland a Section 60 restricted area.

More than 3,000 officers from 12 different forces moved in to stop and search people attempting to shame Britain's biggest polluter – the Drax coal-fired power station near Selby.

The protestors – consisting mainly of families with young children, cyclists, clowns, baton twirlers and a number dressed in white forensic suits – claim the plant produces more CO_2 than 100 small nations.

'They are stopping and searching people again and again, often as little as 10 minutes apart,' said environmental activist and barrister Ralph Smyth.

In some cases, families with children were searched for 'dangerous instruments' up to 20 times in the space of a few hours. 'The notion that people are here for a fight is ridiculous,' Mr Smyth said.

The popular Urban 75 website warns: 'The S60 order is a new police tactic at major demonstrations used effectively to control, subdue and gain personal information about protesters despite having the extraordinarily limited power simply to "stop and search in anticipation of violence".'

Police used the law again when they disrupted a week-long climate change camp at Kingsnorth in Kent, the site of a new coal-fired power station on the Medway estuary.

Assistant Chief Constable Gary Beautridge of Kent Police defended the decision to deploy more police than protestors as a response to 'a small hard core of people…prepared to use criminal tactics and criminal activity'.

'Every year police use the supposed existence of a hardcore minority as justification for the heavy-handedness and every year this hardcore minority fails to materialise,' said the camp's legal spokesman, Kevin Smith.

Around 100 people were arrested over the week, 46 of whom were charged with obstruction in the midst of a field. A Freedom of Information request shows police confiscated children's balloons, tents, a clown's outfit, camping equipment, cycle helmets and bike locks, plastic buckets, bin bags, blankets, soap, banners, leaflets, books, nail clippers and party poppers.

Campaigners complained of the 'constant attention of police helicopters' which disrupted meetings and speeches. Police also impounded vehicles.

'Protestors drew attention to the aggressive tactics of the riot police, who used batons and shields in making arrests. Several protestors were injured when police baton-charged them as they tried to enter a cornfield,' said UKWatch.net.

Liberal Democrat justice spokesman David Howarth criticised the police, saying it was not their job to confiscate banners, walking sticks and children's crayons.

'The idea that it is appropriate to seize ordinary people's property on the off-chance that it might be used to commit a crime is a dangerous precedent,' he warns.

'Almost anything can be invested with sinister intent with enough imagination. I even heard of one case where police confiscated a camper's soap on the basis that it could be used to make them slippery and evade capture by police,' he said. 'This is simply farcical.'

THIS IS DEMOCRACY

'We should not give excuse or quarter to those who claim this country is a police state – that is absolute, utter nonsense. We live in a democracy' – Jack Straw, Secretary of State for Justice and Lord Chancellor.

CONTROL orders, banning orders, gagging orders, house arrest and detention without trial helped give the apartheid regime of South Africa a bad name. What were once seen as intolerable affronts to human dignity are now regarded as necessary tools in the fight for freedom in 21st Century Britain.

The Prevention of Terrorism Act 2005 – which was rushed through both Houses of Parliament in a matter of weeks – has been designed to exempt Britain from Article 5 of the European Convention on Human Rights, a thorny clause that guarantees freedom from arbitrary arrest and detention without trial.

Government lawyers have drafted a law that allows the Home Secretary to place any British citizen or foreign national under house arrest if they are thought to have an 'involvement in terrorism-related activity'.

Known as 'control orders', the terms of house arrest can include electronic tagging, a ban on visitors, limits on movement and a block on communicating via the telephone or internet, and contact with people generally.

House arrest orders have been placed on a number of refugees to Britain and a handful of British citizens. Home Office applications for control orders are held in closed court and the defendants have no right to see or challenge the evidence against them.

The secret evidence does not have to meet the high standards of proof required in criminal cases. But anyone breaching an order is deemed to have committed a criminal offence and can be imprisoned or deported. Control orders last for 12 months and can be renewed indefinitely.

Even the names of those placed under house arrest are kept secret, their only identification to the outside world are a set of initials. The strain for many has led to hunger strikes, mental illness and attempts at suicide. Their plight does not make headlines.

'Do we really want our country to be one that holds men under house arrest – some for more than 20 hours of 24; takes them out of the normal world by allowing them only vetted visitors; confines them to a small geographic area; forbids them internet access; electronically tags them; subjects their homes to random searches day or night without notice; does not tell them the evidence against them, and tries them in a court which hears secret evidence?' asks author Victoria Brittain.

The effect on families can prove devastating with the main bread-winner out of work and relatives, friends and neighbours banned from visiting. Even the children are prevented from using the internet for homework and cannot bring friends home for tea.

Tax payers contribute around £200,000 a year in mortgage and rental fees, council tax and utilities, plus other living expenses, for detainees who can no longer support themselves or their families.

'The whole family is deeply affected by a life constrained by myriad rules, on perpetual alert for the police knock on the door, the invasive search that follows, and the lurking fear of an inadvertent breaking of the rules by speaking to the wrong person, or by a child bringing something forbidden – like a memory stick – home from school,' she says.

Police can also call for control orders on people awaiting trial as a condition for bail, a recent move which Liberty describes as 'police summary justice'.

Former Home Officer minister Tony McNulty justified the use of house arrest as an essential tool in the struggle to defend our freedoms. 'Control orders continue to be an essential tool to protect the public from terrorism, particularly where it is not possible to prosecute individuals for terrorism-related activity and, in the case of foreign nationals, where they cannot be removed from the UK,' he explains.

Liberty, on the other hand, says secret trials and the lack of visible evidence has ended Britain's long-standing legal tenant of innocent until proven guilty and erased one of our proudest traditions – the freedom from arbitrary arrest and detention.

It has also robbed Britain of the moral high-ground. Diplomats protesting at the continuing house arrest of Burma's opposition leader Aung San suu Chi have recently been lectured on our own treatment of 'dissidents'.

'Every aspect of control orders, whether a restriction of movement, association and communication or tagging, curfew or house arrest is punitive,' says Liberty.

The 'non-persons'

QUIETLY and barely observed, the government has introduced measures that can turn anyone of us into a 'non-person'. Imagine if your bank accounts were frozen and you could not withdraw any cash, pay bills or buy food. Even your family could be banned from buying you a pint of milk.

Imagine what life would be like if the Home Secretary suddenly revoked your ID card. And imagine being stripped of your British citizenship. All this is now possible.

One 'non-person' – who for legal reasons can only be known by the initial 'A' – discovered his new status when a 16-page letter from HM Treasury dropped through his letterbox.

'I couldn't make head nor tail of it,' he says. 'But the words that stood out were "terrorist", "al Qaeda" and "United Nations sanctions". To me these are words you only hear in the news.'

One man who can still be named, Londoner Ahmed Salama, did not even receive a letter. When he called HSBC to find out why his mortgage had gone unpaid he was told that his account had been frozen because someone had spotted a 'suspicious' payment.

He had a standing order for £20 a month to a British-based charity for Afghan children.

Both men had been deemed 'al-Qaeda facilitators' and they had been caught by a little-known law that allows the Treasury to freeze their accounts if it suspects they 'may be' involved in terrorist-related activities. No actual evidence is required.

The Treasury says the law, which it describes as a 'robust counter-terrorist finance measure', has helped 'save lives and hold terrorists to account for their actions'.

The law was never debated in Parliament but was issued as an 'order in council' which allows the government to sanction individuals based on a UN security council resolution whereby anyone 'designated' on either the UN or UK watch lists faces 'economic sanctions'.

'The risk of wholly innocent people falling within this category is a very high one,' says Henry Miller of Birnberg Peirce solicitors, which represents a number of people challenging 'freeze' orders:

Around 200 people have so far found their accounts frozen and around 5,000 more are thought to be under observation, many for suspicious 'cross-border payments'.

'Every cross-border payment passes through an electronic system. The cross-border stuff we are particularly interested in,' explains an HSBC official.

Salama, a businessman who held an HSBC account for 11 years, insists he is the victim of mistaken identity. 'My only conclusion is that, with the majority of people being arrested over alleged terrorism offences having the name of 'Ahmed', they think I am one of them or I am laundering money. I can honestly say I am neither,' he says.

'The whole situation has put my whole life in a spin, emotionally and financially. I am a normal Londoner who plays snooker once a week, a little football and cares for the wife and kids. They have taken everything away from me with no real explanation and have not allowed me to pay bills.'

When 'non-person K' tried to challenge his freeze order in court he found that he did not have a leg to stand on. He also discovered that he had fallen into a mysterious world where not even the officials understand the depth of the sanctions and where he can be criminally liable for spending the change in his pockets.

'No one in the household can work because their income would count as the transfer of funds which could be used for my benefit,' he explains. 'I had to phone my solicitor and ask if my son was allowed to buy me milk from the shop,' he says 'The answer was no.'

Henry Miller says those affected have found themselves trapped in a world of confusion. 'I have asked the Treasury how many pairs of shoes a designated person is permitted to purchase,' he says.

'In response, I was informed I had raised 'complex issues

exploring the fringes of what constitutes a basic expense' and that they would have to consult with a minister to answer my question.'

'It sounds amusing, but if you spend too much money or buy one item too many you could be committing a criminal offence, punishable by up to seven years' imprisonment.'

According to writer and broadcaster John Pilger, anyone falling foul of the Home Secretary faces similar sanctions if their compulsory identity card is revoked or suspended.

'Every place that sells alcohol or cigarettes, every Post Office, every pharmacy and every bank will have a National Identity Register (NIR) terminal where you can be asked to "prove who you are",' he say. The loss of the card would effectively cancel a person's life.

'Private business will have full access to the NIR. If you apply for a job, your card will have to be swiped. If you want a London Underground Oyster card, or a supermarket loyalty card, or a telephone line or a mobile phone or an internet account, your ID card will have to be swiped,' he points out.

'The ID card will not be your property and the Home Secretary will have the right to revoke or suspend it at any time without explanation.'

For the ultimate sanction, the Home Secretary has the power to strip British citizenship from people holding dual nationality if it appears 'conducive to the public good' or if they breach anything on the list of 'unacceptable behaviours'.

Clause 56 of the Immigration Asylum and Nationality Act 2006 allows ministers to deport British citizens from the United Kingdom if they hold a second passport and will not be rendered state-less as a result.

'Deprivation on "conducive to the public good" grounds can apply to someone who was born in the UK,' a Home Office spokesperson confirmed.

The Home Office says it does not keep figures on the number of British citizens holding dual nationality.

'Revoking citizenship is a weasel way out,' says writer Sarah

Left. 'Not every citizen is a credit to this nation but when, say, Jeffrey Archer embarrassed the Conservative party by committing criminal acts he was imprisoned. No one mentioned exile.'

Critics say British citizens suspected of committing crimes should be dealt with by the criminal justice system, not stripped of their citizenship, because deporting them only exports the problem for somebody else to deal with. Liberty is especially worried that there appears to be no justification for the new sanction

'Given the severe impact that these proposals would have on individual rights, we would expect the government to have given clear and persuasive explanations about why they are needed. It has not.'

'Vague assertions that these powers are necessary for the prevention of terrorism are unsatisfactory, especially as many of the provisions would apply far beyond the context of counter-terrorism,' the group told MPs in a briefing prior to the Act.

It says Clause 56 will have a 'disproportionate effect on minority ethnic and religious groups' and will 'marginalize certain sectors of the population'.

'We do not believe it would be an effective and proportionate solution to attempt to export the problem by declaring people to be 'non-citizens' so they can be deported,' maintains Liberty.

Secret deaths

JACK STRAW wants to hold inquests in secret if the evidence is deemed a risk to national security or against the public interest. The controversial plan – which could be invoked in cases involving the death of British troops or shootings by police – was earlier dropped from the Counter-Terrorism Act when it met fierce resistance.

Now new plans to keep evidence secret have again alarmed legal rights experts who fear the measures will be used to hide short-comings in equipment or the embarrassment of deaths from friendly fire as well as suppressing sensitive information about the security services.

Parliament's Joint Human Rights Committee describes Mr Straw's plans as 'an astonishing provision' that will hamper adequate and effective investigation into killings by State agents.

'You have only to recall the disgraceful conduct of the inquest into the shooting of Jean Charles de Menezes by the police, the government's acute embarrassment in cases when poorly equipped servicemen are killed on active service, or the deaths of Dr David Kelly and Princess Diana to know that the temptation to suppress public knowledge would be irresistible to Straw and the members of this shoddy, cynical authoritarian regime,' insists *Guardian* columnist Henry Porter.

Under the new proposals, the Home Secretary will have the power to stop a jury being summoned, replace the coroner with an appointee of his or her choosing and bar the Press, public and relatives.

Mr Straw says there is an imperative to change the law because inquests too 'sensitive' for public scrutiny are beginning to back up. So far, there has been no inquest into the deaths of the 52 people killed in the London bombings in July 2005.

Describing the new plans as 'an absolute disgrace', the Coroners' Society says any such system will be open to abuse and could be used to draw a veil over politically inconvenient cases.

Barrister John Cooper believes there is a great risk that the Home Secretary might be tempted to hold inquests in secret 'where matters to be raised are merely embarrassing for the government'.

'The power could be used to undermine a basic fundamental principle of English law – that of open justice,' he says.

The present coroner's system was instituted in 1887, although the office of coroner dates back to 1194.

A spokesman for Jack Straw's office denied secret inquests would dent public confidence in the system. 'These proposed changes will ensure inquests are as thorough as possible by ensuring that the coroner can always examine all material central to the inquests even if the material cannot be disclosed publicly.'

'They will ensure families can have absolute confidence in the conclusion the coroner reaches because the coroner will have had access to all the evidence,' he said.

The Justice Minister says he understands why some people feel 'uncomfortable' with his proposals. 'It's a real difficulty,' he says. 'What we have to do is try and find a way through it.'

Henry Porter is one who feels uncomfortable and far from reassured. 'We have heard this all before and we know about the process of function creep,' he says. 'Once the law is on the statute book ministers and civil servants abuse them.'

'Coroners courts are not part of the State's apparatus,' he points out. 'They belong to the people and it is the public's right to know any evidence that is disclosed during the inquest into a death.'

TREASON

'You see these dictators on their pedestals, surrounded by the bayonets of their soldiers and the truncheons of their police. Yet in their hearts there is unspoken – unspeakable! – fear. They are afraid of words and thoughts! Words spoken abroad, thoughts stirring at home, all the more powerful because they are forbidden' – Winston Churchill.

IF BRITAIN should ever have a fully-fledged authoritarian government or a malevolent dictator they will have a lot to thank New Labour for. Everything is now in place for a ready-made police state. Even the Head of State – HM The Queen – has found herself sidelined as the ultimate protector of the nation.

In the years since 1997, the party has brushed aside age-old checks and balances on the abuse of political power. It has politicised the police and emasculated Parliament.

In just over a decade, the government has undone 100 years of democratic progress says the International Commission of Jurists.

Previous generations would fail to recognise Britain today.

We live in a country where our every movement is observed and every important personal detail is known to the State. Even our homes are no longer our castles.

The governments of Blair and Brown have shown they are afraid of words and thoughts. They have silenced critics and demonstrated intolerance for protest. They have encouraged neighbour to denounce neighbour and recruited others to spy and snoop.

We have seen laws introduced for the specific purpose of tackling terrorism, only to see them used to spy on suspected 'bin criminals'; and we have not batted an eyelid.

We now have secret courts, hearsay evidence, detention without trial and house arrest. We have consistently been robbed of our freedoms and ancient liberties. Churchill must be turning in his grave.

When our island faced a more direct assault on liberty he warned: 'The power of the Executive to cast a man into prison without formulating any charge known to the law, and particularly to deny him the judgment of his peers, is in the highest degree odious and is the foundation of all totalitarian government whether Nazi or Communist.'

Churchill preserved our most cherished rights during a time of the direst emergency. Today, in the topsy-turvy world of New Labour new speak, we are expected to forfeit our freedom for greater safety from an enemy that apparently despises our freedom. It does not make any sense unless we wish to play into the hands of terrorists. We should not have to trade off liberty for security because, in the end, we shall have neither.

According to the former head of M15, Dame Stella Rimington: 'It would be better that the government recognised that there are risks, rather than frightening people in order to be able to pass laws which restrict civil liberties.'

This is 'precisely one of the objects of terrorism', she says, 'that we live in fear and under a police state'.

Simon Davies, a fellow at the London School of Economics, believes so much damage has been done that there is now a 'generational failure of memory' about individual rights.

'People are resigned to their fate,' he says 'They've bought the government's arguments for the "public good". Whenever government says that some intrusion is necessary in the public interest, an entire generation has no clue how to respond, not even intuitively.'

The greatest danger to civil liberties says Daniel Finkelstein of *The Times* is not the repressive laws themselves but their shear quantity.

'We are now passing so many new laws, so quickly, and so many of them are sloppy, that we don't have time to debate them properly or reform them when they go wrong,' he says. 'Parliament is drowning in a sea of legislation.'

Each new law is an unseen brick in a wall; the sheer quantity blinding us to the bigger picture. As Shami Chakrabarti of Liberty warns, 'the small measures of increasing ferocity add up over time to a society of a completely different flavour.'

'If you throw live frogs into a pan of boiling water they will sensibly jump out and save themselves. If you put them in a pan of cold water and gently apply heat until the water boils they will lie in the pan and boil to death,' she explains. 'It's like that.'

The few who noticed the temperature rising have found themselves questioning their own sanity. How could it be possible that in a supposedly open and democratic society, with a free and enquiring Press, we sat silent while everything that made Britain special was stripped away in so short a time?

'Those who understand what has gone on in Britain have the sense of being in one of those nightmares where you are crying out to warn someone of impending danger, but they cannot hear you,' says Henry Porter.

Even our language has been debased to the point where outright attacks on our liberty are accepted in the name of freedom and democracy. Orwell would have been impressed.

Hitler, who abused and distorted the democratic system to his own advantage, would have been impressed at the barefaced cheek of Jacqui Smith, Jack Straw, Gordon Brown and Tony Blair.

In late 2006, the unthinkable very nearly happened. Members of Parliament narrowly avoided voting themselves out of a job completely. Only a few last-minute fixes in the House of Lords prevented the introduction of an Act that would have abolished Parliament itself.

The original and rather dull-sounding Legislative and Regulatory Reform Bill was possibly the most dangerous piece of legislation ever laid before Parliament. It would have handed ministers the power to change any existing law, repeal legislation or introduce new laws without any reference to Parliament.

At the stroke of a pen, a minister could abolish trial by jury, suspend *habeas corpus*, or change any legislation governing the legal system – with the sole exception of the Human Rights Act.

What would have made front-page headlines had it been debated in the Zimbabwe Parliament, went largely unreported in the British Press.

The Bill, which was quickly dubbed the Abolition of Parliament Bill, would have seen '700 years of democracy and the rule of law thrown away in a heartbeat,' says the Save Parliament campaign.

'What's left of the *Magna Carta*, the foundation of just about all modern democracies, would have been finally gone and our Parliament, which has influenced democratic systems all over the world, would just be a footnote in history,' it says.

The Bill's stated purpose was to help cut red tape but legal experts Clifford Chance quickly spotted that the new law would 'usurp' the power of Parliament and remove 'Parliamentary scrutiny for primary legislation'.

Remarkably, while the minister piloting the legislation, Jim

Murphy, tried to bamboozle Parliament, just two journalists were watching events from the gallery. Henry Porter was one of them.

'Watching, I reflected that this was truly how democracy is extinguished,' he said. 'Not with guns and bombs, but from the inside by officials and politicians who deceive with guile and who no longer pretend to countenance the higher interests of the constitution.'

A revised version was eventually passed by Parliament with most of the dangerous elements removed. Britain came within an inch of handing unfettered power to ministers, giving them the ability to create new powers of arrest, sack judges and even override the five-year Parliamentary term and cling to office indefinitely.

Government legislators, miffed at the rebuff, took comfort in earlier having passed the Civil Contingencies Act 2004 with minimal opposition and almost as great affect. Known as the 'Henry VIII' power because it grants 'absolute' authority to ministers, the law that ostensibly deals with clean water supplies, fire services and health and safety in times of emergency, also hands State officials undreamt of power.

Previously, only the Queen could declare a state of emergency. Now ministers can assume state of emergency powers without having to declare a state of emergency. By issuing an 'order' that a 'situation' or 'event' exists or is about to exist, mainland Britain can be placed under similar emergency measures to those of Northern Ireland.

The move has been described as 'highly dangerous' by constitutional law experts Wade & Phillips, who point out that: 'It places in the hands of politicians, the government of the day, a power previously exercised by the head of State – the monarch.'

The law firm warns of yet more function creep when it says the Act allows ministers enormous discretion to 'mix ongoing business in normal times with powers that are intended to deal with peacetime emergencies'. While previous state of emergencies could only be declared for 30-day periods, the new powers 'appear to be indefinite until revoked'.

The woolly words in Clause 18 of the Act define an 'emergency' as 'an event or situation' which threatens serious damage to human welfare, the environment or the security of the United Kingdom. The law also provides for new powers to protect banks and the money supply.

Clause 21.2.h. grants special powers to the State for 'protecting or restoring the activities of banks and other financial institutions'.

During its discussion stage, Parliament's Joint Committee on the Bill expressed 'extreme concern', saying: 'In the wrong hands this could be used to remove all past legislation which makes up the statutory patchwork of the British Constitution.'

Under the Act, anyone sanctioned by the State can requisition or confiscate property, including buildings and personal possessions. Telephone services can be terminated, websites closed down or blocked and the Press and television subject to full censorship.

Movement to or from a 'specified place' can be prohibited, as can assemblies and other 'specified activities' – thought to include the banning of organisations. Failure to comply with a direct order or obstructing 'a person in the performance of a function' can result in imprisonment of up to three months or a fine.

'The effect would be to ban the right to demonstrate and the right of free movement,' says Wade & Phillips. 'These powers would not just ban protest and travel but...introduce new criminal offences to counter any dissent.'

We now face the prospect of armed troops deployed on the streets of mainland Britain and special peoples' courts to dispense summary justice. Entire towns and cities can be closed off, preventing movement in or out. All it takes is a minister to 'suspect' that an 'event' either in Britain or overseas is about to happen and 'at a stroke democracy could be replaced by totalitarianism,' warns Tony Bunyan, editor of Statewatch.

'The powers available to the government and State agencies

would be truly draconian,' he cautions. 'This is Britain's Patriot Act.'

With a mismanaged economy, ever-rising unemployment and an embittered population, the government – which seemingly failed to spot the 'downturn' – had the foresight to introduce sufficient laws to safeguard the money supply and maintain the *status quo* while clamping a lid on virtually every aspect of public protest.

No one can deny any government the right to emergency powers. What is wrong here is that the government has artfully removed safeguards on abuse from the previous Act and, worst still, given ministers the right to use these powers on a mix-and-match basis to be added to the police arsenal any time the government feels threatened.

By by-passing the Queen – the final check and balance to Parliamentary abuse – the State has assumed absolute power over our lives.

This drip, drip, drip of government legislation has had a soporific effect on all of us. We have signalled that we are prepared to stomach any interference in our lives; and the government has taken full advantage of the tolerance and good-nature that lies at the heart of the British character.

But had a new administration introduced all these repressive laws over-night – this treasonable assault on Constitution and country – we would not have been so complacent

We would now be in a state of civil war.